How the BEST TEACHERS Avoid the *20* Most Common Teaching Mistakes

Elizabeth Breaux

EYE ON EDUCATION
6 DEPOT WAY WEST, SUITE 106
LARCHMONT, NY 10538
(914) 833–0551
(914) 833–0761 fax
www.eyeoneducation.com

Library of Congress Cataloging-in-Publication Data

Breaux, Elizabeth, 1961-
  How the best teachers avoid the 20 most common teaching mistakes / Elizabeth Breaux.
    p. cm.
  ISBN 978-1-59667-109-6
  1. Teacher-student relationships. 2. Effective teaching. 3. Classroom management. I. Title.
  LB1033.B637 2008
  371.102--dc22

                                                          2008046881

10 9 8 7 6 5 4 3 2

Editorial and production services provided by
Hypertext Book and Journal Services
738 Saltillo St., San Antonio, TX 78207-6953 (210-227-6055)

Also Available from EYE ON EDUCATION

Classroom Management Simplified!
Elizabeth Breaux

How to Reach and Teach ALL Students—Simplified!
Elizabeth Breaux

REAL Teachers, REAL Challenges, REAL Solutions:
25 Ways to Handle the Challenges of the Classroom Effectively
Annette and Elizabeth Breaux

101 Answers for New Teachers and Their Mentors:
Effective Teaching Tips for Daily Classroom Use
Annette L. Breaux

Seven Simple Secrets:
What the Best Teachers Know and Do!
Annette L. Breaux and Todd Whitaker

The Poetry of Annette Breaux
Annette L. Breaux

What Great Teachers Do Differently:
14 Things That Matter Most
Todd Whitaker

Classroom Motivation From A to Z:
How To Engage Your Students in Learning
Barbara R. Blackburn

Rigor is NOT a Four-Letter Word
Barbara R. Blackburn

The High-Trust Classroom:
Raising Achievement from the Inside Out
Lonnie Moore

Teach Me—I Dare You!
Brough, Bergman, and Holt

Dedication

This book is dedicated to Mrs. Marge Barker: my former ninth-grade teacher, my inspiration, my mentor, my current editor, and my lifelong friend. Through example you molded me into the teacher that I am today. Thank you for your kind yet always firm nature, your insistence on excellence, your gentle heart, your open mind, and your undying devotion to the thousands of students who have walked through your classroom door. I am so fortunate, proud, and honored to have been one of them. I love you.

Meet the Author

Elizabeth Breaux is one of the most practical, down-to-earth, informative, and entertaining authors and speakers in education today. She has spoken to audiences across the country where she leaves them laughing, crying, and certain that they have chosen the right profession—teaching. She is the author of three best-selling books: *Classroom Management—SIMPLIFIED*, *How to Reach and Teach ALL Students—SIMPLIFIED*, and the coauthor with her sister Annette Breaux of *Real Teachers, Real Challenges, Real Solutions*.

A former curriculum coordinator and classroom teacher, she currently trains and supports new teachers in Lafayette, LA. She is also one of the coordinators of TIPS, an induction program for new teachers in Lafayette, LA. In addition, she trains assessors for the Louisiana Department of Education and is an international presenter for the Bureau of Education and Research.

Liz has taught and worked with at-risk students for 24 years and believes that there is not a more challenging and rewarding job in the world. Her message has always been a simple one: *"I cannot teach my students until I reach my students."*

For information on bringing Elizabeth Breaux to your school or district, contact her at 337-654-0040.

Table of Contents

Foreword

Make no mistake about it … CHILDREN WATCH OUR EVERY MOVE! They are masters at exploiting our weaknesses. They know precisely when and how to "push our buttons." They are at times the screwdrivers. We, at times, are the screws.

This may sound harsh, but reality usually is. And unfortunately, this is the reality in many of our classrooms. Too often, students are the ones in control. After 24 years of dealing with some of the toughest challenges and classroom situations, I have come to the conclusion that most breakdowns in the classroom can be traced to one or more of what I refer to as the common teaching mistakes that we have all made—mistakes that could have been rectified or completely avoided.

After reading this book, you will feel more in control of your own classroom. You will feel a new sense of empowerment. With your newfound empowerment, you will become a more highly respected and effective teacher. Remember that you chose this profession because you love children above all. You continue to choose the profession every day as you make life-changing decisions. This book will give you the tools to make the decisions that will positively impact the lives of every student you teach. Your influence is lasting. Make sure it's a positive one.

> *Mistakes I've made, both grave and small*
> *(In that I'm not alone)*
> *But the ones that harmed me most of all*
> *Were the ones I failed to own.*
>
> —Elizabeth Breaux

Introduction

What I've Learned About Teaching

- I've learned that teaching is the hardest, but most rewarding work I will ever do.
- I've learned that the job description is only the beginning of a teacher's responsibilities.
- I've learned that students are all different, yet innately quite the same.
- I've learned that all students are reachable and teachable individuals.
- I've learned that students crave structure and guidance and yearn for leaders who are assertive and in control.
- I've learned that students detest weakness in adults.
- I've learned that students will find and exploit our every weakness.
- I've learned that a calm, caring, and structured environment is necessary for human growth.
- I've learned that students will respect authority, if that authority is fair, kind, consistent, caring, and genuine.
- I've learned that many of the breakdowns in the classroom can be traced to one of the common mistakes made on the part of the teacher.
- I've learned that when students "win," they really lose.
- I've learned that the quality of the teacher is the determining factor in the success of the students.

How to Use This Book

This book will take you into the classrooms of many teachers who face the same challenges that all of today's teachers must conquer. The typical mistakes will be presented in the section, *Defining the Mistake.* This will be followed by *Examples of the Mistake.* Next will be a segment on *How to Correct the Mistake,* followed by another on *How to Avoid the Mistake.* All will culminate in a *Bottom Line* or chapter summary.

As you read through each chapter, you will undoubtedly be reminded of the actions of your former teachers, your fellow teachers, and yourself. My wish for you is that you will feel validated, self-assured, and eager to take additional steps toward becoming a better teacher with each passing day and year.

What This Book Will Do For You

- ◆ If you want to take charge of yourself and your classroom,
- ◆ If you want to destress your teaching experience,
- ◆ If you want to create a calm, caring, and structured environment,
- ◆ If you want to truly make a difference in the life of any student,
- ◆ If you want to reach each student so that you can teach each student,
- ◆ If you want to stop second-guessing your own actions and reactions,
- ◆ If you want to be the determining factor in the success of your students

… then this book is the one for you!

If I Already Knew

If I already knew what I think that I know
Or if even I knew that I really don't know
To quite the extent that needn't I learn
What I already think not to be a concern

You should already know that my age is no reason
To assume that I'm wise or in any way seasoned
What I say, as you've learned, is directly impaired
By my dire desire to pretend not to care.

I firmly believe that I shouldn't need teachers
I shouldn't need parents or mentors or preachers
Science, Biology, Algebra II
Just why I need those I haven't a clue

So assume, if you will, that never I've heard
Of the rules of the school (though it sounds so absurd)
And tell me exactly what I'm to expect
And what you require is what you will get!

—Elizabeth Breaux

Mistake 1: Assuming Students Already Know

Defining the Mistake

One of the first and worst mistakes teachers make is assuming that our students already know our expectations. We often assume that the older students are, the more they should already know. Some of us even assume that they can read our minds and that in failing to do so they are disobeying or disrespecting us!

Often, in our haste to start teaching, we simply fail to lay the proper foundation, forgetting that the foundation is the groundwork on which teaching takes place. Without it, teaching cannot be effective. We are so anxious to start teaching the content that we neglect to teach the basic rules and procedures that will allow for more efficient and effective teaching and learning in the content area.

How many times have you either made or heard a fellow teacher make statements similar to these?

- ◆ "I'm not going to tell him that it is disrespectful to talk while I'm talking! He's in the seventh grade and should know that by now!"
- ◆ "I should not have to tell eighth graders to walk quietly in the hallway."
- ◆ "Tell a fifth grader that she must remain seated unless given permission to do otherwise? I don't think so!"
- ◆ "Waste precious time 'teaching' rules and procedures? We might not finish the book!"

This mistake of assuming that they already know can be one of the most tragic mistakes that we make in our classroom because if we assume that they already know, then we will naturally take the defensive when they fail to do as we expect.

Example of the Mistake

I remember the very first day of my teaching career like it was yesterday (although I've tried hard to forget it). I had finished college in May and was planning to start teaching during the fall semester. Sleeping soundly on that early June morning and not having to get up any time soon were luxuries I had earned. However, those luxuries were much shorter-lived than I had expected.

The phone rang at 7:30 A.M.; I, of course, was sound asleep. I answered it and, to my surprise, the principal from the high school across the street from my apartment complex was calling in search of a teacher to teach the summer school English I class. When the teacher originally hired to teach the class had not shown up, the principal had called the school board office in search of someone else. Because I had recently applied for a job in the public school system, he was able to acquire my name and contact information from my application.

"I've got 36 students seated here in the gymnasium and no one to teach them," he said. "Would you be interested in the position?" Still half asleep, and probably thinking I was merely dreaming, I told him I'd be there shortly. The next thing I remember vividly was being given a key to a classroom, the promise of some textbooks as soon as they could be located, an apology for not having a teacher's manual to go with the course, and 36 sleepy, apathetic teenagers staring dazedly into the space that was the gymnasium. The rest is a blur. Suffice it to say that although I did manage to "swim" through that summer school teaching experience, it wasn't pretty. I spent most of my time kicking and splashing, but made it safely to the side each day. I didn't drown, but was barely afloat the entire time.

In retrospect, I was able to see my mistake(s) quite clearly, the biggest having been my expectation that high-school students should have already known the rules of the game. Because of that, I had neglected to teach them to play by MY rules! I had just expected that they would, since I was in charge, and had then become frustrated each time that they did not! How dare they? Didn't they known that I WAS THE TEACHER?

Correcting the Mistake

My students were not following procedures as I had expected. It had become worse with each passing week, until finally I felt I had no recourse. I was furious at these students who should have been old enough to know what I had expected, and at myself for not recognizing much earlier that what had happened had been within my control. I had chosen to allow the students to implement procedures their way in my classroom. I had chosen to assume that because of their ages they should have been able to read my mind. I had chosen to conclude that the reason they were not behaving as I'd expected was probably due to the fact that they were, of course, all past failures. Every one of them was retaking this course during the summer session because they had failed it during the previous school year. I had relinquished my power to the students and blamed them for not using it according to my plan.

Many of you have probably found yourselves in similar situations. For every step forward, you've taken 10 steps backward. You've begged, pleaded, punished, fussed, referred students to the office, and called parents, but nothing has worked. You're exhausted and have little fight left in you.

Question: What do you do now?

Answer: Own it yourself. Apologize to your students for your mistake of not teaching the procedure properly. Apologize for your inconsistencies in properly implementing the procedures. Then ask for their help in starting over. Ask students if they would mind not having class and just talking for a while about a few procedures instead. Then, start over! The great thing about teaching is that we can have a "Monday" on any day of the week and at any time of the year we choose.

Take some time to revamp. After your discussion with your students, proceed to actually TEACH them through explanation and modeling exactly what you expect. Once you've clearly explained the proper implementation of a procedure, PRACTICE it. Allow the students to try it with your guidance. Once you are satisfied with the practice session, begin to IMPLEMENT each procedure.

Now, here is the part that is most difficult for many of us. It is absolutely critical that you implement the procedures with utter consistency for routines to develop properly. If you allow the students to begin implementing procedures according to their interpretation instead of yours, everyone loses. Consistent implementation is the key, and its success is firmly in the hands of the teacher.

Avoiding the Mistake

In order to avoid the mistake, assume that your students have no inkling as to what your expectations are. The first few days of school should be spent laying the foundation. I always began my year by doing the following:

- ◆ **Apologizing** to the students for the vast number of expectations.
- ◆ **Sympathizing** with them regarding the reality that expectations vary from classroom to classroom.
- ◆ **Assuring** students that I fully expected them to struggle with meeting all expectations initially, and that failing to do so would not be considered failure, but simply a reason to revisit the expectation.

Then I could begin establishing initial rules and procedures as they would be implemented from that day forward. Before doing so, however, I needed a predetermined list of rules and procedures and a plan for teaching each one of these on the first few days of school.

Make a list of those that are most important for the smooth, organized, efficient functioning of your classroom. Your list might look something like the following one. A more detailed explanation of how to "Teach, Practice, and Implement" these can be found in my book *Classroom Management Simplified* (2005).

1. Entering the Classroom
2. Tardiness
3. Implementing Bell Work
4. Sharpening Pencils
5. Using Classroom Materials/Supplies
6. Distributing/Collecting of Class Materials
7. Getting the Students' Attention
8. Getting the Teacher's Attention
9. Participation
10. Completing Homework Assignments
11. Talking in Class (Use of Codes)
12. Group Work
13. Discarding Trash
14. Conducting Parent Conferences
15. Calling Home
16. Requesting Bathroom Privileges
17. Taking a Test

Begin on day one by starting with #1 on your list. *Teach* (tell, show, model, etc.) the students exactly what you expect. Then, *Practice* with the students. Allow them to role-play. Allow them to make mistakes! That's right … actually ask them to make mistakes! Make it fun. They will enjoy it regardless of age/grade level. Use this practice time to rectify mistakes, so that when you move on to the *Implementation* phase, you simply need to remind, reinforce, and remain utterly consistent!

Bottom Line

There are as many different sets of rules, procedures, and general expectations as there are classrooms in any given school. Students are not mind-readers. (We must be ever thankful for that!) Identify your expectations before the beginning of school and spend the first few days teaching, practicing, and implementing those procedures. Be willing to revisit and revamp whenever necessary. Understand that the well-managed classroom that runs efficiently and effectively is not possible without the guidance of the teacher. The teacher is the key. Make a firm commitment to yourself and to your students not to waver in regard to the proper implementation. Remain firm yet kind, helpful yet unbending, consistent yet not controlling! And that brings us to *Mistake #2: Attempting to Control.*

Mistake 2:
Attempting to Control

Defining the Mistake

If we allow ourselves to believe that we can control others, we are setting our own stages for failure! If in our efforts to gain control of our classrooms, our students, or our lives in general, we forfeit control of ourselves, we have lost the very thing for which we are striving: control! We must each believe and say to ourselves, "The only person I will ever control is me!"

Each of us has witnessed numerous examples of the loss of self-control. Sadly, many of those examples have taken place in our schools. The obvious ones are those where teachers have ultimately given up and resigned their teaching positions. Those are the situations that ended positively, for at least those teachers bowed out gracefully. The saddest of situations are those where the teachers continued to strive for control without realizing that their tactics were flawed. Their efforts, consequently, continued to be in vain. Most often those efforts focused on controlling others, which is never possible if one has not gained control of oneself. If I cannot control my own actions and reactions, there is no chance of my ever being in control of the actions and reaction of those within my tutelage. My students look to me for guidance and example. Good or bad, my example is the lead that they will follow.

The greatest teacher I ever had stood all of about 5 feet tall and weighed (possibly) 100 pounds soaking wet. Her name was Mrs. Barker and those of us fortunate to have been her students were wise to have used her example later in our own lives. She was the teacher who was always in control. She was in control of her classroom, the cafeteria, the gymnasium, and the entire campus. Her presence was motivation for those around her to maintain self-control. She led by example, never losing control of herself under the guise of trying to control others, yet by doing so, she seemed to be in control of EVERYTHING! Those who entered her classroom exited having gained self-worth, self-control, self-discipline, and an immense amount of knowledge of the English language. I realized many years later that the reason Mrs. Barker seemed to be in control of everything was that she was in total control of the only one over whom she ever had the possibility of ever controlling: HERSELF!

Example of the Mistake

The mistake of losing control comes wrapped in many different packages, yet the content is always the same: failure to have perfected the skill of self-control. The following examples might sound familiar:

1. Mr. Nice Guy wants to be everyone's friend. He wants the students to like him, so his focus in addressing situations is always done with this goal in mind. He has expectations but is not consistent in relaying them to his students for fear that all may not agree with him. He has class rules but seldom implements consequences so as not to upset his students. What he has failed to realize is that his actions, or lack thereof, have caused the classroom environment to become hostile because of all the inconsistencies. Students who are given consequences view him as being unfair. His attempts to be "Mr. Nice Guy" have rendered him incapable of controlling situations because he has failed to control his own actions and reactions in a manner that would afford him respect from his students.

2. Mrs. Negative, in her "efforts" to live up to her name, has managed to completely lose the control for which she is striving. Her methods of strong-arming her students into following her directions include the use of screaming, belittling, sarcasm, threatening, and several other well-known methods of negative reinforcement. Mrs. Negative is known for exhibiting very little control over her own actions. She can be heard screaming through the walls of a closed-door classroom and openly in other areas of the campus. She has been heard saying, on more than one occasion, that she is "forced to use these methods because they are the only ones that the students will respond to." Doesn't she realize that if these methods really worked, she would no longer be "forced" to implement them?

3. Mrs. Office Referral relies on the administration to control her students. She believes that this is the only thing that "works with these students." Because she has failed to build teacher-student relationships, ones where boundaries are built and lived within, her classes are always out of control. Because she has failed to teach students the procedures which would allow for the efficient running of her classroom, she is forced to extinguish fires on a daily basis. Because she has failed to clearly establish classroom rules where consequences other than office referrals are clearly stated and implemented consistently, students continue to "push her buttons." Removing students from the classroom becomes what seems to be the only viable option. Everyone views Mrs. Office Referral as having no control. That description is accurate because she has neglected to gain control of her own actions and reactions.

4. Mr. Hammer controls everything and everyone (or so he thinks). He has a rule for every rule in his classroom. He has a plan for how the administration should deal with those who don't follow his rules. He bullies other teachers (especially those much younger than he). He

bullies the students through his relentless use of humiliation and sarcasm. He believes that his tactics work because he always gets precisely that for which he searches: the upper hand. Mr. Hammer, of course, is the only one who views himself through those glasses. Others see him as the inflexible, rigid, unscrupulous person that he is. The students fear him, but they don't learn much from him. (If being scared into silence were the definition of discipline, his classes would be considered very well-disciplined.) The teachers have no respect for him. The administration loathes him. The parents pray that their children won't be placed in his class. He, however, is in total control of his own actions, regardless of how appalling they seem to others. It is through his actions (those that he alone controls) that he and his tactics are viewed as reprehensible to others. It is because of his actions that he has never been and will never be an effective, respected teacher.

Correcting the Mistake

Most mistakes are fixable, but not until they are acknowledged. Once identified and acknowledged, they can be dealt with in an appropriate manner. You may feel as though you have lost your edge or that you have never even acquired an "edge!" Again, identify what you have been doing before you try to fix it. Acknowledgment followed by an apology will usually open the door to negotiation. Remember that once you have gained control of your own actions you can negotiate just about anything in your favor!

I can remember making promises to my students. My first promise was that I would speak to them in the same manner in which I would prefer to be addressed. Another was that I would never expect of them what I would not expect of myself. By allowing my students to hold me accountable for my actions, I was able to hold them accountable for their actions. In fact, they even evolved into young people who would hold themselves accountable for their own actions. All of this, of course, had evolved from the example of a teacher who held herself accountable for her own actions in the first place, a teacher who could be highly respected by students and peers alike, a teacher who always seemed to be in control of just about any situation!

Avoiding the Mistake

The only way to keep a controlling personality under control is to submit to the belief that gaining control of others is never an option. The only viable option is that of gaining control of myself. I must be willing to admit that I am the only person over whom I will ever have any control. Once I acquire control of my own actions and reactions, those around me will view that quality with respect. Because of that respect, they will then gain control of their own actions and reactions to the everyday things that go on within a classroom. Only then am I seemingly in control of everything!

To avoid making the mistake, teachers must first become familiar with and be in agreement with the following characteristics of both teachers who are in control and those who are controlling. (The following is taken from my book, *How to Reach and Teach ALL Students—Simplified* [2007, pp. 16-17])

Teachers who are in control:

♦ would never dream of getting into a power struggle with anyone;

♦ treat others with the utmost respect and expect the same in return;

♦ are consistent in the implementation of rules and procedures;

♦ would never use shame or embarrassment as a way to gain control;

♦ realize that dislike forms a barrier between teacher and student, making any exchange of knowledge virtually impossible;

♦ do not *ever* raise their voices in anger, but maintain a calm demeanor in all situations;

♦ are firm yet kind;

♦ have high expectations and a zero tolerance policy for unacceptable behavior. The penalty/consequence, however, always fits the "crime" and the implementation is consistent;

♦ realize that they are *constant models* of what they can expect from others, thus they always behave accordingly;

♦ are masters at spotting the positives and bringing them to the forefront; and

♦ use the administration as a last resort for themselves as the prime disciplinarian and classroom manager.

Teachers who are controlling

♦ often get into power struggles with students;

♦ are disrespectful of students and are disrespected by students;

- use embarrassment and shame as a way to deal with students;
- are often inconsistent in the implementation of rules and procedures, causing students to view them as being unfair;
- seldom make positive home contacts;
- tend to believe that they are victims of students;
- often scream at students;
- have a serious dislike for those who are in control;
- are masters at spotting the negatives; and
- use office referrals as scare tactics and often count on the administration to force the students to behave appropriately.

In order to avoid the mistake, take an honest inventory of your past behaviors and interactions with your students. Which ones best characterize you? Which can you perfect and which can you avoid?

Bottom Line

The bottom line is quite a simple one. Gain control of yourself by managing your actions and your reactions. Be a model of self-control. Accept that you will make mistakes and be willing to hold yourself accountable for those mistakes. Allow others to hold you accountable for your mistakes as well. Then and only then will you seemingly have control over many of life's situations. Remember that you can never control others. You can, however, effect change in others by being in control of yourself!

Lost Within a Shout

You yelled at me and I yelled back
What else was there to do?
We yelled some more, our throats got sore
And the tension grew and grew
And finally, in exhaustion, we both ran out of steam
Left standing in embarrassment, no pride left to redeem
What point is there in thinking that to be "right" we must
Keep pushing on till all involved just lose respect and trust?
Maybe if we'd listened, we could have met half way
Let's talk next time and really hear what the other has to say
For if we both could do that, maybe we'd find out
That never has a point been made when lost within a shout!

—Annette Breaux
(From *Real Teachers, Real Challenges, Real Solutions*)

Mistake 3: Engaging in Power Struggles

Defining the Mistake

NOTE: After reading *"Mistake 2: Attempting to Control,"* this chapter, *"Mistake 3: Engaging in Power Struggles"* may initially appear to be redundant. The two do go hand in hand, yet the latter is a specific action of those who have a tendency toward attempting to control, so it therefore merits attention of its own.

When contemplating a power struggle, remember this: it takes two! Unless a second is willing to engage, the potential for the struggle evaporates. Anyone attempting to engage in a power struggle needs a second person to add the fuel. Once I choose to engage, I am adding the necessary fuel that will ignite the fire. When I continue to engage, I add the fuel that helps the fire continue to grow and thrive.

Often, without realizing it, we teachers are the ones who engage by adding the fuel needed to start the fire. We sometimes even continue to add the fuel that feeds the fire. We have that power. We can choose to fuel and refuel the fire or to snuff it out altogether. The choice we make will be the determining factor in whether or not the fire withers or rages. This analogy may sound a bit simplistic, but it's accurate. Students will try to engage us, but we always have the upper hand. Our reaction is the determining factor.

Unfortunately, students are not always the initiators of power struggles! Most of them, however, will engage when invited. Don't be the one to send out the invitations; and if invited, please refuse to attend!

Always remember that some issues are simply nonnegotiable. Rules and procedures, for example, if implemented with consistency to be effective should (except in extreme cases that are exceptions) have no room for negotiation. The very minute that the teacher allows negotiation of a matter whose details have already been predetermined, a power struggle is usually imminent. Be careful. You are in control of these situations.

All children need boundaries. If those boundaries are ambiguous, students will try to cross them. It is up to the adult to impose firmly established ones that are nonnegotiable.

Question: How will the students know when an issue is nonnegotiable?
Answer: When the teacher refuses to negotiate!

Example of the Mistake

I was grocery shopping recently and heard a mother shopping with small, noisy, twin boys. Both boys were walking beside the grocery cart. I was behind them and, unfortunately, could not seem to pass them due to the large number of shoppers in the aisle. Every 5 feet or so one of them would grab something from the shelf and throw it into the cart. The mother would yell at them, insisting that they place it back on the shelf. The boys would argue and whine, "Why can't we have it?" With every question asked, the mother responded. With every answer from the mother came a response from the boys. The boys grumbled, while the mother yelled and reprimanded. This went on for several aisles until I was able to make a quick and clean getaway somewhere between the canned peas and the frozen foods!

I had just witnessed two children who had obtained full control over their mother. They had sent out the invitation for a power struggle and she had engaged. I am going to assume that the yelling continued into the parking lot and for the entire ride home. I'll also assume that there were threats of punishment or reprimand either when they arrived home or "if it ever happens again!" I'll also assume that those threats were idle ones, since this behavior did not seem to me, as an observer, to be a first-time occurrence.

Correcting the Mistake

So, after reading the previous example, you are fairly certain that you were the one I saw in the supermarket! (Maybe not the exact one, but your experience with your youngsters has, at times, been eerily similar.)

You also know that those same little devils miraculously become angels when at school. In fact, their teacher marvels at their good behavior. What is she doing that you are not? How can you (as either a parent or teacher) fix this mistake when it seems to have grown to such tremendous proportions?

1. Acknowledge that there is a problem and be willing to take responsibility for it.

2. Know that you are the only one who can rectify the problem. Handing the problem over to Daddy or to the principal might serve as a quick fix, but the situation is ultimately going to be placed back into your own hands where you will have to deal with it.

3. Identify appropriate behaviors for specific situations.

4. Have a meeting. Whether at home with your own children or in your own classroom with your class. Be firm but kind. Explain what you want (rules along with consequences). Model what you want. Have the students practice. Praise them profusely. Correct them when necessary. Have fun.

5. Begin the implementation and remain CONSISTENT! Without consistency, it will not work. Remember that you are the one in charge of

whether or not it is implemented with consistency. DO NOT NEGO-TIATE. Have the child serve the consequence in as close succession to the "crime" as possible. If you miss the opportunity, you will automatically set the wrong precedent: the one that got you in a bind in the first place.

6. On the other hand, look for correct implementation and praise it. Bring it to the forefront. Let them know how proud you are. Tell their parents and other teachers about it in their presence. If you choose to give a tangible reward, do it. Just know that it is not always necessary. I seldom gave tangible rewards to my students. My thanks and praise and constant appreciation of them as my students were the ultimate reward, but there is nothing wrong with a little prize or privilege every now and then.

Avoiding the Mistake

Imagine those same twin boys in the classroom of a teacher who has firmly established boundaries. This teacher is firm yet kind. She is soft-spoken yet always in control. She is the teacher whose rules and procedures have been plainly established. She is the teacher who seems to have all "good kids" every year. She is the teacher who has a class of twenty-seven 6-year-olds instead of just two like the mother in the store! She is the teacher who takes her students to the library. She is the teacher who takes her students into the community. She is the teacher who ALWAYS makes certain to establish procedures and rules along with consequences and rewards before embarking on any outing. She is the teacher who teaches her students how to, when to, if to, and what happens if the "how to's," the "when to's," or the "if to's" are not ADHERED to! She is the teacher who reminds often and gives thanks and praise whenever the opportunity presents itself. She is the teacher who brags about the awesome behavior of her students to parents and fellow teachers. She is the teacher who never engages in a power struggle with a child or allows for negotiation over a matter that has clearly been predetermined as nonnegotiable. She is the teacher who implements the consequence immediately whenever a rule is broken. She is the teacher who never raises her voice but remains cool at all times. She is also the parent whom shoppers would marvel at as opposed to trying to escape from if ever they were caught behind her in a supermarket aisle!

How do we avoid making the mistake of engaging in a power struggle with our own students? The answer seems quite simple: just refuse to do it! But let's go a step further. How can we virtually remove the possibility of students (or our own children) ever even attempting to engage us in a power struggle? That would be the ultimate objective. Wouldn't it be great if the opportunity to engage in a power struggle never presented itself? Here are some tips on how to establish just that.

1. Make certain that rules and procedures are firmly established, whether in a classroom setting, a home setting, or some other real-world setting.

2. Establish boundaries that, if crossed, will merit a consequence.

3. Discuss the boundaries/rules and their consequences in detail. Teach them, practice them, and then implement them precisely as taught. (Try to make the consequence one that can be implemented as soon as possible after the infraction.)

4. Deliver the consequence as soon as possible in the event that the behavior requires one.

5. Deliver the consequence every time. This is how students learn whether your boundaries are solid or flimsy!

6. Deliver the consequence in a mild, firm, yet controlled manner. Do not negotiate, or you lose!

7. Offer rewards for proper implementation. Remember that rewards don't always have to be tangible. The best teachers offer thanks and praise and then spread the good news to others in the presence of the child. This is often the best reward that any student can receive.

8. If offering tangible rewards, DO NOT PRESENT THE REWARD if it is not merited! Teachers often feel sorry for a student who has broken the rule and end up giving him/her the reward anyway! This is when you lose your power because you have just handed it over to the child.

Remember that in any situation that is nonnegotiable, don't negotiate. It's that simple. If there is a consequence for an infraction, implement it as stated. Do not bargain, or the students will begin to believe that negotiation/bargaining is an option. Be consistent. It is truly within your power to choose to continue or not to continue proper implementation on a consistent basis.

Bottom Line

Power struggles occur when two people feel that there is an issue that is open for negotiation. A person who does not have the skills to negotiate an issue in an adult-like fashion may resort to a heightened tone of voice, name calling, accusations, and so on, all of which will actually prevent the issue from being resolved. If the skills necessary to resolve the issue do not exist, the two adversaries begin vying for power (hence the screaming, name-calling, accusing, etc.). The truth is that in student-teacher and parent-child relationships, some issues are simply *nonnegotiable!*

Many children do not know how to handle conflicting viewpoints. Too often, the incorrect way has been modeled for them at home, and unfortunately, at school. They have seen far too many adults handle conflict in inappropriate ways, and that's all they know. Teachers must absolutely and unconditionally *never* allow power struggles to occur between themselves and their students.

It's really quite simple. It takes two to tango! Students will try to engage you. That's a given. You are the one with the choice. If you engage, the battle begins. And, there is no such thing as winning the battle. Power struggles are never won even though those who engage do so with the intent of winning. Everyone loses. Don't ever be the one to lead your troops into a losing battle.

What Is It You Said?

What is it you said, that you hate what I'm teaching?
You hate all the class work, the homework, the preaching?
And never before have you been so removed
From the lessons the school board has strictly approved?
I work you too hard and that is appalling?
You've referred to my talks with your parents as galling?
You titter and tatter, you gaze and you stare—
I know there's a student inside you somewhere!
How dare I attempt to have you speak out?
When I beg your attention you grumble and pout—
You whine and complain, you whimper and gripe—
(That smirk on your face I am dying to wipe!)
So now back to teaching, hither I go—
There's a god out there somewhere, this surely I know.

—Elizabeth Breaux

Mistake 4: Taking Student Behavior Personally

Defining the Mistake

Teachers and their students, no matter what the age or age difference, do not view matters of the world through the same lenses. Subject matter that is important to the teacher is not always viewed by the student as having value. If teachers mistake those negative views as personal attacks, effective teaching and learning is often forfeited.

I remember an incident that took place at the beginning of my teaching career, where several students expressed to me, in no uncertain terms, that they "hated to write." I was appalled. I was their English teacher. They had to write. I loved writing, and I needed for them to love writing. If they couldn't love it, something was wrong with me. Me, Me, Me, Me! I was internalizing the comment and taking it to a personal level. It didn't feel good, and I was not happy! While I was articulating my disgust during a therapy session (the therapists being the other teachers who happened to be in the lounge that day), a very wise veteran teacher responded with the following message that immediately enabled me to move to another level in my teaching experience.

Always remember that the word "hate" is usually used as a synonym for the word "fear." We tend to fear things that we have not yet accomplished or mastered. If we're not good at it, it feels like "hate!" Think about all of the things that you are not skillful in doing. You probably don't like to do them. It just doesn't feel good."

She continued by giving me some examples that could pertain to me and to my students. A light bulb turned on for me. I got it!

"Poor readers," she went on to say, "are often the ones who don't like to read. Nonathletic students are usually the ones who hate going to physical education class. We adults who are not in shape hate to exercise!"

She really had me thinking then. "So what do I do for those students?" I asked her.

"Make them successful!" She answered. "It's the only way to pique an interest. Give them a tiny taste of success, and they'll want more. Just make certain to help them to achieve that success on their own level. Not on your level, or my level, or on the level of *others in the class*. We learn on our own levels. But whatever you do," she added, "don't allow them to become stuck at that level. Move them forward quickly, making certain that the first success is allowed to breed more and more successes, at higher and higher levels, until you have them where you want them to be, or at least very close to it. That's what teaching is all about. You can't take it personally. Now stop griping and get back to teaching!"

That was the day I stopped taking things personally. I've never forgotten her words of wisdom. I've just looked at the "hate" as a "fear" of something and then set out on my journey to make the students successful. Remove the fear by making them successful, and that dreaded "hate" word can be removed from their vocabulary!

Example of the Mistake

You've planned a great lesson. It's a beautiful day. You're anxious for class to begin because you know the students will be completely engaged and enthralled. All are present. The tardy bell rings. You introduce the lesson with an enormous smile on your face and enthusiasm in your voice, when a student in the back of the room blurts out, "Why do we have to do this?"

You are devastated, humiliated, mortified, and defeated. This was your day. How dare he take it from you? How dare he criticize your hard work? How dare he be unappreciative of your efforts? Who is this evil little heathen and what have you done to deserve him?

His words have severely affected you, and your demeanor shows it. Your blood is boiling, and your mouth is moving in response to his comment. You can't seem to stop your words. They are out before they cross your mind and then descend onto your students. Because your person has been "attacked," your person attacks in revenge, actually answering the question ("Why do we have to do this?"). You are now in battle mode and your words, of course, must outdo his. Class has ended before it began. All of this happened because you allowed yourself to take it all personally. You mistook his question as an attack on you, thus your reaction was imminent.

Correcting the Mistake

Now consider the alternative to having taken the "Why do we have to do this?" question personally. Instead of taking the remark as a personal attack and engaging in the power struggle over why the material is actually relevant, you instead pause and consider the question, asking yourself the following questions:

1. Have I made the real-life connection between the material and the students' lives?
2. Is the material appropriate to the students' learning levels, or do the students already loathe the material because they know they are not good at it?

Then, ask the following question of the student: "Why do you ask?" Accept the student's answer to the question and ask for input from others. Hold a class discussion. The students will notice that you value their opinions and will become much more open-minded in regard to the planned lesson.

My greatest teaching challenge came when I was given the task of teaching the alternative students. These were eighth-grade students who were all two grade levels behind. Some were four or five learning levels behind. The challenge was to have them pass the state test, which of course was on an eighth-grade level. After 3 weeks of "I hate's" from most of my students in reference to just about everything I'd presented to them, I had all but given up. These students needed to be able to write a 200-word essay on the state test in 7 months, yet many could barely write a complete sentence. I truly felt that we all were going to be hopeless failures.

I was going home depleted and discouraged every night. Their failures were my failures, and I took that quite personally. I remembered the words of my mentor, *"The only way to get them where they need to be is to start them where they are."*

We began immediately, and there was plenty to do. The first lesson involved writing sentences. That's right. Complete sentences! I had been so busy trying to cajole them into writing essays, that I'd forgotten that the fear of the unknown (the essay) was causing them to use the dreaded word: HATE! Amazingly and expectantly they could each write a complete sentence after one short lesson. I did, however, commend them for that and quickly moved on.

Next was the task of mastering the art of writing the paragraph, and none were proficient at that. After several weeks of very intense writing sessions, all students felt comfortable at successfully writing a well-structured paragraph. They were experiencing success; thus, the fear (hate) was subsiding. They didn't even realize what was happening.

I, on the other hand, knew precisely what was occurring. I no longer internalized the occasional *"I hate this"* or *"I hate that."* I had learned to see it as a signal of a necessary task of much greater proportions: that of removing that hate or fear by making them successful. By doing that, I was able to stop making the mistake of taking students' fear or hate as a sign of my own shortcomings.

Avoiding the Mistake

In order to avoid taking students' actions, reactions, comments and innuendoes personally, I must first believe that they are never a direct attack on me. Failure at anything often erects defenses. Attack is imminent. The teacher is often the target. I must remember the words of my mentor, *"hate is another word for fear,"* and must know that I can always remove the fear. How do I remove that fear? I remove it by making my students successful. How do I make them successful? I do so by challenging them at their own levels, recognizing their accomplishments, reinforcing their accomplishments, and then moving them to the next level. I must remember that success breeds more success.

I used to begin my year by asking students to make a list of the things they hated ("feared" although I didn't use that term yet) doing. I made a list of my own. We shared our lists with one another. I must admit that I initiated and had us complete this activity as much for myself as for my students. I also found it to be a great "get to know you" activity for the beginning of the school year. It was fun, interesting, engaging, and sometimes sobering. Many of us shared our feelings with one another that we found were commonplace among others. It initiated the start of our "family." Coincidently, once that family evolved, personal attacks were few.

Bottom Line

- *Hate* is a word often used to articulate *fear*.
- Remember that it is human nature to be afraid of (or hate) being placed in situations where a successful outcome is doubtful.
- Forget the "I hate's." Instead, strive to remove the fear by making your students successful.
- Teach students at their level, whatever that may be.
- Be liberal with your praise.
- Nothing breeds success like a little success, and that little success can become the foundation for great accomplishments.

I'm not opposed to learning; in fact that's why I'm here
I've listened and I've questioned, yet the reason's still unclear

If this is how it's done, and that is how it's made
Then how am I to use it when in front of me it's laid

I wrote down every figure, every fact, and every line
I even had my mother call it out a thousand times

I used an acronym to memorize it for the test
Then on the test I set it in its final place to rest

I'm sure that there's a reason why my teacher made me learn it
I'd try to clarify it if I only could discern it

It came and went so quickly that so little I recall
Even though just days ago I thought I knew it all

One day when I am in a bind, and need to make a move
Will I know how to use it since the learning was removed?

—Elizabeth Breaux

Mistake 5: Foregoing the Real-Life Connection

Defining the Mistake

Students must believe that the subject matter being taught has relevance in their lives. They must believe that it has value outside of the classroom. For example, how will memorizing historical dates be beneficial in their lives if they do not understand how the long-term effects of those occurrences are felt today? How will memorizing unfamiliar words seem relevant if those words are not shown and studied in context? How will memorizing mathematical formulas seem pertinent if those formulas are not applied using a real-life, everyday situation?

Learning in the real world is hands-on. We learn while we do. We understand once we have tried, failed, revamped, and tried again. We make mistakes, correct them, and then strive to become better. Each task, each trial, and each new tribulation is wrought with lessons that have true meaning, or our efforts would be in vain and, therefore, would have little relevance in our lives. That which is irrelevant is usually deemed unimportant. That which is unimportant matters not, so we give it little, if any credence.

Real-life teaching is quite simply the act of relating the subject matter to the learner's life. It is intent on creating a real-life connection which in turn piques curiosity. It is venturing out and away from the textbook and into the real world. (A textbook is a wonderful guide and supplement, but it is not the teacher.) A lesson that is relevant is creative, unique, interesting, engaging, meaningful, and fun. It does not lend itself to boredom and redundancy, because in real life, things are always changing.

In real life our attention to certain matters is given for a variety of reasons, but seldom because it is demanded. The same applies in any classroom setting. As a student, regardless of age, will I consider something worthy of my attention because

1. someone I trust (teacher, friend, relative) says that it is?
2. the media says that it is?
3. knowing it is expected of someone my age?
4. it's going to be on next week's test?
5. if I don't finish it now, I'll have to finish it for homework?
6. I see its relevance in my own life?

If you chose number 6, you understand fully why we learn. You understand what it takes to gain an interest in a new topic. You know that in order to open a mind to learning, that mind must be able to assimilate a topic's relevance and yearn to integrate it into what is already known and understood.

In other words, if you want my attention, relate the subject matter to my life in some way. Only then will I be learning and retaining instead of memorizing and forgetting.

Unfortunately, many of us teach the way we were taught.

- ◆ We spit out facts, figures, and formulas.
- ◆ Students copy endless amounts of notes (sometimes simply transferring words from one document to another).
- ◆ We assign chapters to read and questions to answer.
- ◆ We give enough work to keep fingers busy and mouths closed for hours on end.
- ◆ We create study guides that mimic the test. Just study the guide and you'll "learn" the material.
- ◆ We give stacks of worksheets to be completed in a designated amount of time. We have extra worksheets readily available for the early finishers.

All of this and some students are still lazy, apathetic, and uncaring. We don't understand their lack of interest. We loathe their lethargy and laziness and wonder what must be wrong with their parents. We ponder the source of the indifference and then we continue teaching the same way. Nothing changes and we wonder why.

The following is taken from my book, *How to Reach and Teach ALL Students—Simplified* (2007, p. 102).

Tips for Making the Lesson Real

1. Remember that you are the teacher. The supplemental materials (text book, work books, programs, etc.) are only tools. They will only come to life when you make them real.

2. Before beginning a lesson, any lesson, relate it to real life, but make sure it's the students' real life (past, present, or immediate foreseeable future).

3. Tell your students stories to which they can relate. It can be a story of something that happened to other students, to you, or to someone they don't know. If they can relate to it in some way, you've "got 'em!"

4. Allow students to make connections between the text and themselves, the text to a previously read text, and the text to the world.

5. Use hands-on activities as much as possible. Students respond much better when they are able to manipulate something. On-task behavior will improve dramatically.

6. Take them on field trips. Even a trip around the campus to relate something to an aspect of your lesson can be immensely effective.

7. Start looking at how you taught things to your own children and model your lessons after that. The truth is that in real life, we don't need a textbook, handbook, or worksheet. We just get right in there and we do it!

8. Remember that all disciplines are interrelated. For example, you can include historical matter in the planning and teaching of an English lesson. Additionally, industrial arts, music, and physical education are perfect venues for teaching math concepts in real-life formats.

Examples of the Mistake

Do any of you remember "Vocabulary Day?" I do … quite vividly. The memory of it from my days in school was so lucid that I began incorporating it in my own classroom exactly as my teachers had done. Because I was teaching middle school reading at the time, Monday seemed the perfect day. Every Monday the lesson in Ms. Breaux's class was exactly the same:

1. Take out your notebook and insert today's date.
2. Take out your textbook.
3. Take out your dictionary.
4. Today's list of vocabulary words is on the board. Complete it.
5. Any not completed in class must be completed as homework.

That's it! No teaching! No learning!

This was not intentional, however. I truly believed that until the students had learned the meanings of the unfamiliar vocabulary, reading the story was not possible. I had forgotten to make the real-life connection, thus all Mondays in my classroom were a complete waste of time since very little, if any, learning was taking place.

I recently observed a young teacher of mathematics as he struggled to teach his students the formula for finding the area of a circle. He stood at his board, pointing to a circle, then pointing to the formula. Students plugged numbers into the formula for circles of varying sizes. It seemed almost robotic. I wondered if the students had any idea as to the relevance of all of this. Looking at their faces made me doubtful that they did.

Watching them made me remember all of the days when I had sat in very similar classes. I can remember wondering how and if I would ever use this.

The answer came to me many years later in my life when I developed a love for landscaping and realized that many of those formulas I had learned many years before could actually be useful. The problem was that I couldn't remember them because I'd never actually learned them. I had memorized them for a test and probably done quite well. Since the connection to real life had never been made for me, they were soon forgotten. Remembering them for future use was simply not necessary, since at the time I had not foreseen a situation in my life where they might be useful.

Correcting the Mistake

After several years of Vocabulary Days, I began contemplating their importance and merit.

- Were students really learning anything on those long, drawn-out, boring, time-consuming days?
- Was there another way to actually learn the meanings of unfamiliar words?
- Had my students really been learning anything at all?
- Was I really teaching or was I handing that job over to a dictionary?
- Is it imperative that we know the meaning of every word before we read a story?
- Is it possible that by experiencing unfamiliar words in context, the students will deduce the meanings of the words? *Isn't this what we do in real-life?*

I'm actually embarrassed to admit it, but until that moment of clarity, I hadn't given it much thought. Once I did, my method of teaching changed forever. Why not, I thought, teach this and everything else the way I would if I were teaching it to one of my own children (or anyone, for that matter) in a real-life situation?

For example, if I were recommending a recently read novel to a friend, I would not suggest that the friend complete a 25-word vocabulary assignment before beginning the novel! That would be absurd! Knowing that there were several words that were unfamiliar to me and might be to her, I still would never consider such a recommendation. I already know that while reading novels, I encounter some difficult passages, some that I read and reread. For example, when I read, I attack unfamiliar vocabulary in several ways:

1. I skip right over them if they aren't critical to the overall interpretation the author was trying to convey.

2. I use clues to make sense of the words as they are used in the actual context.

3. If neither of the above meets my need to know, I'll pull out my trusted old dictionary and look it up!

If that's how we would do it in our own real-life situations, why not teach it that way in our classrooms? Imagine the following interaction between a teacher and his/her class:

Teacher: Open your text to the story on page 27. Let's read the first paragraph together. (Reading and discussing take place. The teacher relates an event to one in his/her life. Students offer examples from their own lives.)

Teacher: Based on what little we know thus far, what do you think might happen next?

Students: Several give answers.

Teacher: I see what seems to be a difficult word that was just used in line 3. Can anyone give us a definition of that word?"

Students: Several give logical (some illogical) answers. (The teacher writes each on the board. Students discuss and the teacher eliminates all that are agreed upon as being incorrect. Two remain.)

Teacher: Now that we have narrowed the possibilities to two, let's see what the dictionary has to say.

Students: All open their own dictionaries and locate the word.

Teacher: I see that there are four different definitions of that word. Which do you think is the correct one?

Students: Answer and discuss until the correct definition is agreed on and verified by the teacher.

Teacher: Let's jot that one down in our notebooks.

Notice that the students are still using a dictionary and copying the definition into their notebooks, only now it has meaning. Now, they actually understand what they are writing. In fact, the note-taking now serves as reinforcement instead of mindless busywork (as it had on those notoriously meaningless Mondays).

Let's consider how the math teacher (from Examples of the Mistake) could have given a real-life twist to the lesson on finding the area of a circle.

Teacher:	Now that we are all outside, we are going to plant some flowers around the trees that were recently planted on campus. Here we have some old bricks that we will use as a border. We will prepare the area first before planting. Today, I would like you to determine the number of bricks that are needed to encircle each tree. Here is what I would like for you to do. (The teacher places students in groups of four. Each group is assigned to a tree. The teacher tells students that the trunk will serve as the center of the circle. Students must determine the circumference of the circle when given only the radius, which is different for each tree.)
Teacher:	Now that you know the length of the radius, plug that into the formula for finding the circumference of your circle.
Students:	All students complete the computation, using the formula that was given to them, $C = \pi \times d$, to determine the circumference of their circle.
Teacher:	Now that you know the circumference, you will need to gather enough bricks to use as your border. Each brick is eight inches long. Determine the amount of bricks that you will need for your tree."
Students:	All students complete the task.

The students are using the same formula that has always been used to find the circumference of a circle. However, when the teacher uses a real-life format to teach the concept, the students will be a great deal more likely to remember it and use it for the rest of their lives!

Avoiding the Mistake

The best way to avoid this mistake is to take a very close inventory of your teaching strategies.

♦ How many of them are strategies that you would use in a real-life situation?

♦ Which are the ones that are most engaging for your students?

♦ Which elicit the greatest amount of interest from your students?

♦ Which promote on-task behaviors from most, if not all, of your students?

Make that real-life connection, regardless of subject matter. Tailor your strategies so that they are most closely related to real-life ones. Vary your teaching strategies. Redundancy leads to boredom for you and your students! Following are some examples of teaching strategies that lend themselves to a more real-life way of teaching and learning:

- ♦ Problem Solving
- ♦ Role Playing
- ♦ Brainstorming
- ♦ Use of Graphic Organizers
- ♦ Cooperative Grouping
- ♦ Story-Telling
- ♦ Small-Group Instruction
- ♦ Open-Ended Questioning
- ♦ Hands-On Teaching and Learning
- ♦ Guided Reading
- ♦ Shared Reading
- ♦ Peer Tutoring
- ♦ Team Teaching
- ♦ Discussions
- ♦ Debate

Bottom Line

If we can relate a topic to our own lives in some way, we will be much more willing to bring it into our consciousness as something that we can use in some way. On the other hand, that which we do not view as being important or valid in our lives today, we may reject as being immaterial to us. We're just not interested if we cannot make a connection.

Helping students make that connection is a difficult task at best. Without that connection, however, teaching occurs in a vacuum, with the teacher sometimes existing alone inside of the vacuum while the students float around somewhere else in space! Unfortunately, that scenario is one that promotes little learning.

None of us want to teach to four walls, yet we see it happening in far too many of our classrooms. The teacher has the power to change that. The information may exist in the textbooks, workbooks, computer programs, and so on, but the teacher is the source that brings it all to life. Don't exist in a lifeless classroom. Instead, plan lessons that the students can relate to their own lives, lessons that are engaging and exciting, lessons that encourage participation and prevent off-task behaviors, lessons that, at the end of the day, make us proud to call ourselves "Teachers."

The Sum of My Parts

If the sum of my parts is what makes me my whole
And your parts are different from mine (I've been told)
Then your parts assembled should not look like mine
And mine should, of course, confirm separate designs.

Designs that are different, too often in practice
Regarded as one using similar tactics
Expecting one whole to react as the other
When one is his own and the second another.

If this sounds confusing then you should be me
Struggling and striving and yearning to see
The world through the parts that belong to the sum
A whole that's not I and I cannot become!

—Elizabeth Breaux

Mistake 6:
Teaching to the Whole

Defining the Mistake

NOTE: It is by design that this chapter, "Teaching to the Whole," follows the chapter, "Foregoing the Real-Life Connection," because those teachers who teach with the real-life connection in mind naturally teach with individual differences in mind. In real life we already know that children do not learn if we use the same methods for all of them. Somehow, however, we seem to forget that when we step into our classrooms. Portions of this chapter are taken from my book, *How to Reach and Teach ALL Students—Simplified* (2007, pp. 113-122).

We are all different. We are different in appearance, in dress, in likes, and dislikes. We come from different backgrounds. We are of different religions and ethnic groups. None of us dispute these facts. Like it or not, everyone is not just like us! That includes learning styles, learning preferences, learning abilities, and so forth. Yet if I, the teacher, choose only to teach students in one way, using one style and limited teaching strategies, I am excluding all whose needs are different from mine or from everyone else's.

With this knowledge, we must realize and "buy in" to the need for accommodating the many differences in learning styles by structuring our lessons so that instruction is differentiated and meets the needs of all students. "But I have 26 students in my class," you say. "Am I to create a different lesson for each one?" Of course not! That would not be feasible in any setting. What you can do, however, is to create an environment where there is a blend of different methods of instruction, to include whole-class, individual groups, or individuals. You can vary your instructional strategies and your activities so that you are reaching all students.

We must distance ourselves from the old one-size-fits-all theory. In every classroom, in every school, students function on different learning levels. Unfortunately, grade level and actual learning level are not always synonymous. Assuming that we are in agreement on this, what would happen if we took a class of students on various learning levels, and taught them at the same level? What would happen, unfortunately, is that we would teach only the ones at that level. Invariably, some would be bored because they would feel as though they were being spoken down to, and some would be lost because they had not yet arrived at that higher level.

Teaching is not for the faint of heart; that's why we chose to teach. We knew we were ready for the challenge. And it *is* challenging. None of us would dispute that. If you are a teacher who is unfamiliar or uncomfortable with the concept of differentiating your instruction, or you find it extremely challenging because you think that it's just too much work, or that the students can't handle it, the list of Tips for Accommodating the Differences under the "Avoiding the Mistake" section is sure to help. Please give it a try.

Example of the Mistake

Let's remember that the objective is to *differentiate our instruction and activities so as to accommodate the many differences in our students*. Let's remember that students need our assistance. Let's remember that if a student is failing, something is obviously not working!

Let's look at a list of some strategies/activities that simply don't work.

- ◆ Any activity where everyone is doing the same thing in the same way all or most of the time.
- ◆ Lack of variety in teaching strategies.
- ◆ Lack of variety in activities.
- ◆ Lack of knowledge of the individual needs of students.
- ◆ Busy-work that requires no assistance from the teacher.
- ◆ Lack of individualized assessment practices.

Unfortunately for me, and for my students at the time, the above list brings to mind the teacher that I was 25 years ago when I first began my career. In the last chapter I revealed, reluctantly, that back then most Mondays in my classroom were what I now refer to as vocabulary days, which consisted of meaningless, mindless copying from one source to another. Invariably, the same students were my behavior problems on those days. Because I was teaching the way I had probably been taught and, thus, didn't know any better, the remaining days in many of the weeks in my classroom were probably as ill-planned as those Mondays were. The concept of individualized instruction simply did not exist. Unless a student had an extreme exceptionality that required individual assistance by a source other than me, the primary teacher, I used the same activities for everyone except for those fortunate few for whom I had been given a specific accommodations plan. If one read silently, all read silently. If one answered questions, all answered questions. When assessments were designed, only one was designed! "All for one and one for all!" The obvious problem with that approach was revealed in the outcomes.

Correcting the Mistake

This may be one of the most difficult mistakes to rectify. Teaching is already a monumental task, one that requires more from one individual than does any other profession in the universe. (This, of course, is my opinion, which I am certain would be corroborated by any teacher!) The bottom line is quite simple, yet ironically it is our most difficult task: *Teachers must teach individuals, not classes.*

In my experience, I have found three teaching strategies in particular to be highly effective for individualizing instruction in most class settings. They are also, in my opinion, the least difficult to execute.

1. Cooperative Grouping
2. Centers or Workstations
3. Team Teaching

Cooperative Grouping

Keep in mind that when using cooperative grouping as a teaching strategy, you must be flexible (makeup of groups should be continuously changing), you must be organized, and you must also be an impeccable classroom manager! I hear it all of the time and am frankly more and more disgusted every time I do: "My kids are too bad to work in groups. I just give them enough to keep them busy on their own." One teacher recently said to me, "My kids can't handle all of that fancy stuff." My question to her would be this: "Is it really the kids who can't handle the fancy stuff?"

Authentic cooperative grouping is truly a cooperative effort. Group members are given individualized responsibilities (assignments). These assignments require interaction and cooperation from all group members, but each student is performing a different task. Tasks/responsibilities should be geared to individual needs, strengths, learning styles, and so on.

Centers or Workstations

When you are creating centers/workstations, attention to individual needs, variety, and interest is of utmost importance. Students are grouped and placed at individual centers for a given amount of time, enough to complete the task. At the end of that amount of time, groups move to another station where they attend to a different task or assignment. In other words, students may be learning the same concept, but in a variety of different formats. It is not only an excellent way to meet the needs of all individuals, but it is a brilliant approach to keeping all students on task! The most difficult element in implementing this strategy comes in the planning phase. If this activity is well planned, however, the teacher can take the role of facilitator, monitoring and giving individual attention as needed.

Team Teaching

Teaching as a team is not a new concept, yet it is one that is not often utilized. When employed in a carefully calculated, well-planned manner, it can be invaluable. When teachers, facilitators, teacher assistants, adult tutors, and so on, teach as one unit, accomplishments can be monumental. This too, of course, takes concerted planning, but the rewards can be innumerable. When team teaching is executed properly, the teachers can tend to the more individualized needs of the students. When the teacher groups students according to needs, activities and assessments can be geared toward those needs.

Avoiding the Mistake

With calculated planning and forethought, the mistake of teaching only to the whole group can be avoided. It's not easy, but what else about our profession is? You will find, however, that once perfected, it will become second nature. Teaching individuals with individual needs in mind will become second nature. You will do it without even realizing what you are doing.

Tips for Accommodating the Differences

- Become very well **organized**!
- Become a great **classroom manager**.
- Learn about your students. If you've been teaching the class for a while, you already know them fairly well. If it's the beginning of the year, have them complete a **"Learning Styles" inventory**. There are some great ones out there.
- Talk to your students' former teachers and review previous assessment data.
- **Ask** your students. They'll be happy to share with you their likes and dislikes relating to teaching methods, class activities, learning environments, study practices, and so on.
- Make a list of some of the **teaching strategies** that you use most frequently and then add some that you have been reluctant to use. Focus on implementing a plethora of different ones. (A list of strategies was given in the previous chapter.)
- **Plan well** for the lesson. Have all materials and activities in order and readily available.

- If you are going to use a strategy that you have not yet used, be ready to "Teach, Practice, and Implement" the procedures for doing so.
- Be willing to **create varied group assignments** where everyone in the group is given a different task or assignment!
- If you are going to use **stations** in your room for the first time, be ready to "Teach, Practice, and Implement" the procedures for doing so. Stations allow for materials to be presented to students in a variety of ways.
- If you are going to use **peer assistance** or **peer tutoring** for the first time, be ready to "Teach, Practice, and Implement" the procedures for doing so.
- Prepare activities that are **hands-on** and **activity based**.
- Make certain that **assessments are individualized**.
- Use **rubrics for assessing** students' work.
- Make certain that **you are actively involved** at all times.
- Do some research on **"Learning Styles," "Multiple Intelligences,"** and **"Differentiated Instruction."** You'll obtain some great information and ideas for implementing new strategies and techniques.

Bottom Line

Teaching to the whole assumes that all students are identical in learning levels, learning styles, and learning abilities. This is never the case in any classroom setting. We must differentiate our instruction in order to afford students many different options and opportunities for absorbing, digesting, assimilating, understanding, and using ideas and information. We must provide an environment where students of different abilities can learn within the same class setting.

To embrace the idea that to accommodate all the differences, we must differentiate our instruction, we must first affirm in our own minds that students come to us with varying backgrounds of knowledge, interests, learning styles, and readiness. They are not all in the same place, at the same time. If they were, teaching would not only be the easiest job in the world; it would also be the most boring!

Accommodating all students in one class setting is not an easy or small undertaking. The weak of heart, mind, and will, could never do it. That's why *we* are teachers. *We want to teach, and we want our students to learn. All of them. Not only the ones who are just like us. We are committed to doing whatever it takes to achieve that goal.*

I planned a lesson I assumed
Would last for sixty minutes,
But when it failed to fill the slot
I didn't seek to mend it.

I let it go and wouldn't you know
The outcome was quite frightful:
My angels turned to villains-
Malicious, horrid, spiteful!

"Settle down, behave yourselves!
What do you think you're doing?
Get back to your seats and do not speak!"
My raging pleas came spewing.

Then to my rescue, my last reprieve
In the knick of time befell,
To save the day from come what may,
My friend, my pal, the bell!

—Elizabeth Breaux

Mistake 7: Allowing for Unstructured Time

Defining the Mistake

First, let's look at a list of responses from a group of 28 ninth graders when asked to define what "free time" in the classroom meant to them.

- ♦ "It's usually wasted time."
- ♦ "What we do is up to us, within reason of course."
- ♦ "We're supposed to do homework, read, do work for other classes, whatever."
- ♦ "Do you really want to know?"
- ♦ "I can tell you what it means to me, or I can tell you what it means to most students. Which would you like to hear?"
- ♦ "It's dangerous for me. I'm sort of the class clown and free time is 'prime time' for me!"
- ♦ "Most teachers use it to grade papers (or whatever else they do) while we're supposed to keep ourselves busy. Most of us find something constructive to do. Not always, but most of the time."
- ♦ "It's the first few minutes and the last few minutes of every class period."
- ♦ "Time to catch some ZZZZZZs!"
- ♦ "That's when I wake up. This teacher is so boring."

Their teacher, of course, had defined the term free time in a clearly more precise fashion. Unfortunately, his definition did not match that of any of his students.

So let's assume that in most classrooms, free time is perceived more or less as idle time. Attempts to define it would be futile, since its worth is little. Still, it is commonplace in many classrooms, and the result is the loss of countless, precious, instructional minutes.

Ironically, however, most teachers today when asked whether or not there is enough time in the school day to accomplish all that is currently expected will answer with a resounding "NO!" They will tell you that class periods are not nearly long enough. Ask if any of them could accomplish what they are currently able to accomplish if the school year were shortened by several days or weeks, and they will laugh at you. If all teachers had the opportunity to survey a number of classrooms (other than their own), they'd find that many teachers unintentionally squander minutes haphazardly, not realizing that those minutes balloon into what culminates in days, or even weeks of lost instructional time.

Call it what you may, unstructured time too often lends itself to becoming wasted time. Whether we are purposely giving free time to our students, or simply unintentionally squandering away priceless minutes, we are losing something that can never be retrieved. We teachers have no time to waste.

Examples of the Mistake

Mrs. Jack in the Box was obviously born with springs on her legs and feet. This is the only feasible explanation for her ability to spring from the chair of her desk to the front of her classroom, readily assuming the "teaching" stance in less than 3 seconds. She has performed this feat so many times in her career that she is known to be, hands down, the best in her school. Ask any administrator who has ever entered her room at any point during a class period, and they will admit that they have never actually caught her teaching.

Mrs. Jack in the Box is notorious for referring students to the office for disciplinary reasons. It seems that most students in her classes are referred at least once, if not many times, during the year. If Mrs. Jack in the Box would become conscious of the fact that the enormous amount of idle time incurred by her students is contributing to the disorder, unrest, and unruly behaviors, she could fix the mistake. Of course, fixing the mistake would entail saturating each class period with effective instruction, and this seems to be precisely what Mrs. Jack in the Box is trying to avoid.

Mr. Flimsy, unlike Mrs. Jack in the Box, truly wants to effectively instruct his classes. He is not lazy. He is not seeking to avoid performing the job that he was hired to carry out. He is always well-planned and prepared. Unfortunately, he has not mastered the art of implementing a good classroom management plan, one that would allow time for effective instruction. Many of his students are late for class, thus causing the initial minutes of class to be lost on a daily basis. He begs and bargains with them to arrive in a timely fashion, but his lack of an assertive, authoritative demeanor makes his attempts futile. Once he is able to secure the attention of all students, that attentiveness is short-lived. His reactive, as opposed to proactive, methods of teaching cause what was intended to be instructional time to become disciplinary time. By the end of the period, Mr. Flimsy is exhausted. He usually gives the students 5 to 10 minutes of free time at the end of each class period. He uses that time to gather his wits for the next group of students. Ultimately, his inability to manage his classes renders his instructional planning fruitless. Mr. Flimsy's intentions, though noble, are thwarted by his lack of classroom management skills. This can be rectified, if the problem is acknowledged and the proper help is sought.

Correcting the Mistake

If you know, or are fairly certain, that there is too much wasted time in your classroom, whatever the cause, you've already taken the first step toward rectifying the problem: recognizing that there is one. In my work with new teachers I tell them that there is a guaranteed way to know whether or not they are losing precious time in their classrooms.

Wear a stopwatch for a day or more. Start it when effective instruction is initiated. Do not start your watch when the bell rings indicating the commencement of instruction unless effective instruction also begins at that time. Each time that instruction is interrupted, for whatever reason, stop the watch. Start it again when effective instruction resumes. Be cognizant of all transitional periods, and any other interruptions of the instructional environment so that the watch can be stopped and started again when instruction resumes. At the end of the period, compare the time on your watch to the actual time allotment for that class period.

This can be a huge wake-up call for many teachers. Most of us don't realize how much of our valuable time is lost in small increments, and how easily avoidable the loss actually is. Seeing the final number is usually a bit shocking to some teachers, but it's also a terrific starting point. The challenge now comes in the endeavor to shorten the amount of lost time, thus gaining more minutes which can be utilized for instruction. One of the teachers with whom I was working even made a game out of it, where students became participants. The outcome was amazing.

Once you've determined that instructional time is being lost, you must know the reason(s):

1. Are you not planning for an entire class period worth of instruction? Do your lessons seem to take longer than the period allows or have you finished the lesson with too much time to spare?

2. Do you often find yourself actually using the words "free time?" Are you intentionally giving students idle time at the end or at any time during the class period?

3. Are you losing time due to a lack of a proper classroom management plan?

4. Are you lazy? (Sorry, but if we don't acknowledge it, we can't fix it!) Are you giving loads of busy work and free time in order to free yourself from the task at hand: teaching?

Now that you've acknowledged the problem and determined the reason(s), rectifying it (them) is possible. Each of the previous four reasons can be easily fixed, once acknowledged, of course.

Avoiding the Mistake

1. Become a good classroom manager. Teach, practice, and implement rules and procedures until your class can run like that well-oiled machine.

2. Plan effectively. Always plan more than you might need. It's better to resume and complete the lesson on the next day, than to waste time today.

3. Get out of your chair! Teach from everywhere. Students should not know from which area of the room you normally teach.

4. Get rid of free time. Students should be busy learning, and the teacher should be busy teaching, all of the time.

When training new teachers, I advise them to teach, every single day, as though they were being observed by a supervisor from the school board. There should be no difference in the way they teach when they are being observed, as opposed to when they are alone with their students. If they would do something differently during an announced observation, then they should do it that way on any given day.

Let's use Mrs. Jack in the Box as a prime example. Each time an observer walks into her room, she jumps up and begins teaching. If she thought that she was doing precisely what she was supposed to be doing, she would have no reason to make such an abrupt change each time an observer walks into the room. Teachers who are actually doing their jobs won't even flinch when an unannounced observer enters their rooms. They don't miss a stride. They don't appear startled and taken by surprise as does Mrs. Jack in the Box.

Bottom Line

Unstructured time too often becomes wasted time. Whether we are purposely giving free time to our students, or simply squandering away priceless minutes, we are losing something that can never be retrieved.

Teach from bell to bell! With such a short amount of time allotted for the accomplishment of the daunting tasks that we are given in today's classrooms, wasting time is simply not an option. Don't waste what is so immensely valuable.

Where was it that I placed it
When I laid it safely down
Somewhere where I knew for sure
It could be quickly found
Now finding it is proving
To be quite a daunting task
The urgency is mounting
I've got to find it fast
I know that it is safe at hand
But which hand I'm not sure
It's not in this one or in that
(Is it in one of yours?)
I've overturned the garbage bins
I've tousled every pile
I've ruffled through each drawer three times
And emptied every file
I've blamed it on the students
My husband and my son
I'd probably blame it on the dog
If only I had one
Now to the boss's office
I boldly make my way
Rehearsing every line that I've
Prepared myself to say
Concede defeat is what I'll do
I'll just apologize.

"You turned that in last Friday
Did you not realize?"

—Elizabeth Breaux

Mistake 8:
Failing to Organize

Defining the Mistake

My grandmother used to say, *"A place for everything, and everything in its place. A cluttered environment yields a cluttered mind."* I've learned that by living according to those two old adages, life can become much less stressful.

If I want to create a stress-free classroom environment, one that can be a breeding ground for learning, I must organize the environment so that obstacles to the learning process are removed. Learning cannot take place in a chaotic atmosphere. Therefore, I must become a master of organization before I can become the master of my classroom.

Consider this: if we are disorganized, we cannot command organization from our students. If the teacher is disorganized, the students will naturally follow suit. Our expectations must be reinforced and reflected in our actions. It's absurd to think that we can expect from others what we do not require of ourselves.

Have you ever walked into a classroom where clutter seems to permeate every inch of the room? Because of my work with new teachers, I am in and out of many classrooms, and I can tell you without reservation that a cluttered, messy, disorganized classroom environment is usually a chaotic environment that is reflective of fragmented, disjointed teaching and learning. They go hand in hand.

I'm certainly not implying that there are not some disorganized teachers out there who are (or have the potential to be) good teachers. What I am saying is that if these good teachers became better organized by removing the confusion caused by the unnecessary havoc, they'd be *better* teachers!

Ultimately, learning suffers dramatically in a disorganized, disorderly, chaotic environment. The good news is that the reverse is also true. Students really do love an organized learning environment. They want and crave structure. They need a leader to provide this for them, and we must be those leaders. It's up to the teacher to get the organizational ball rolling!

Example of the Mistake

Mr. Laston invited me to come to his fifth-grade language arts class to do a model lesson. This is something that I absolutely love doing now that I no longer teach my own classes. I've known Mr. Laston for years, because we used to teach in the same school. So, let me give you a little background information on him in order to set the stage for this example.

Mr. Laston truly loves teaching. He's been in the profession for over 20 years now, and anyone who knows him will tell you that he loves his job.

During the years that he and I taught in the same school, I knew that he was a good teacher, even though I had seldom entered his classroom during a lesson. I knew, the same way we all know, who the good teachers are in our schools:

- We watch them on campus with their students.

- We attend faculty meetings and other functions with them and notice that their words and actions clearly illustrate that they are committed to their profession and to their students.

- We know that they are the first to volunteer whenever help is needed for anything on campus.

- They are the ones who arrive early and leave late.

- We hear their conversations with others and notice that their comments about their students are always positive.

- They always seem to be planning something new and exciting for their students.

- We walk near their classrooms and notice that they are always teaching and interacting with their students.

- They have a wonderful rapport with their students, their peers, and the administration.

- Their students are usually highly successful.

Mr. Laston possessed all of these wonderful qualities. He did have one major flaw, however: He was a pig! I mean that only in the "messy and disorganized" sense of the word. He was by all means one of the nicest people I'd ever met. I had ventured into his classroom only a couple of times, through sheer necessity. Disheveled is the most polite term that I can think of to describe it, so I'll use that. Let me assure you there are adjectives that would be much more suitable to describe it, but much less kind. On those few ventures into his tattered domain, I could not help but wonder how much more effective he would be if he could just become organized. He already possessed some of the most awesome qualities that any teacher can possess, yet, because of the muddled environment, his potential to be much more efficient and effective might never be discovered.

Needless to say, when he requested that I teach a lesson to one of his classes, *IN HIS CLASSROOM,* my initial excitement was promptly replaced with angst. "How can I, Ms. 'Arrange, Classify, and Categorize,' possibly teach in such an environment?" I asked myself. The answer was obvious: I COULD NOT! Not wanting to decline his offer, I devised a plan where I could successfully negotiate some terms of the agreement.

Correcting the Mistake

"I would absolutely love the opportunity to teach a lesson to one of your classes," I said. "What lesson did you have in mind?" (He was teaching his students the art of identifying and extracting elements from a story, which happened to be one of my favorite topics to teach.) "I have a terrific lesson I can do on that," I said. "It requires the use of manipulatives, however. It's a very hands-on lesson, so I'll need to prepare the room and the students' desks accordingly."

"No problem," he said. "My room is a little messy."

("Little?" I thought to myself!)

"You might want to come in the afternoon before the lesson," he said.

"Great idea," I replied.

"I'll help you," he offered. "You just tell me what you need and it's done," he said.

This was perfect. The only problem was that cleaning his room had not been part of the bargain, but I had no choice. It was either that or get swallowed up by the mounds of mess while trying to effectively teach the lesson. I arrived after school on the day preceding the lesson equipped with large, yard-sized, heavily reinforced garbage bags, the really expensive ones that truly can handle just about any job. The "set up" (cleaning) process began. I staged the room as though it were my own. We arranged the desks neatly and removed all garbage from the floors and desks. I organized all of the necessary materials and manipulatives, actually placing the ones that would be used at the beginning of the lesson on the students' desks. This is how I had always prepared my classes for such a lesson so as not to waste time distributing materials. Because the flash cards and desk charts, which contained the outline of any story, and individual bags of story elements were all color-coded, the arrangement seemed bright and inviting.

I arrived early the next morning and awaited "my" class. As they began trickling into the room, the expressions on their faces gave way to uncontrollable commenting.

- ♦ "What happened in here?"
- ♦ "Wow! This looks so nice!"
- ♦ "What's all this for? What are we going to do?"
- ♦ Etc., etc., etc.

The lesson commenced, then progressed and developed as planned. Fortunately, the period consisted of a 90-minute block of time, so I had ample time to complete what would have normally taken 2 days to finish. The students truly enjoyed the lesson. They were completely cooperative and obliging when distributing and collecting the various materials that were used for the lesson. I stressed the importance of keeping my materials neat, clean, and free from any markings, as I had been using these same ones for several years and all previous students had treated them with proper respect and care. Everything was done in an orderly manner, according to my requests.

After the students departed, Mr. Laston thanked me with most gracious sincerity.

"What an effective lesson!" he exclaimed. "Would you mind if I borrowed one of your sets of manipulatives so that I can create a class set of my own? I am so anxious to complete this lesson with my other classes!" I happily obliged and welcomed any further invitations to assist in any way I could. As I walked out of the room, Mr. Laston offered one final comment:

"I'm not sure if I can complete this lesson in one 90-minute class period.

I'm amazed at all you were able to accomplish in that amount of time and were still able to make certain that all of the students grasped the concepts quite well. Everything was so well-organized and things just ran so efficiently. One activity flowed right into the next with no wasted time. You were so prepared and the students responded beautifully."

I was thankful that he had noticed. Now I'm just hoping that he'll remember the importance of being well-organized and orderly, and try to incorporate more of it into his daily teaching. He's such an awesome teacher already. If he'd just get organized he could be even better!

Avoiding the Mistake

Following are a few tips that might help you organize your own classroom for ultimate efficiency, thus enabling you to accomplish more in a lesser amount of time. They are taken from a chapter in my book *Classroom Management Simplified* (2005, pp. 5-6).

Tips for Becoming Organized

1. Determine the amount of physical space afforded you and how to best organize that space for maximum efficiency.
2. Arrange your own personal space first. Remember, YOU LIVE THERE!
3. Create rooms/stations within your classroom.
4. Color-code everything!

5. Create bins for everything! Bins should be clearly labeled.

6. Create and display charts for everything: conduct chart, extra points chart, tardy chart, absence chart, and so on. Make certain to assign numbers to students. (Names should never be written on the charts since the information that is being provided and displayed is of a personal nature.)

7. Label and color-code shelves, cubbyholes, and so forth, by class (if you teach more than one class) and then by the materials that are stored there. Students then know what is off-limits to them and what is not. They also know where items "live" in the classroom.

8. Create supply boxes for your students. This works for all grade levels. Fill a small plastic box with necessary classroom supplies (pen, pencil, scissors, glue, ruler, eraser, crayons, compass, protractor, highlighter, calculator, etc.). Place one in each desk. Write the name of every student who sits in that desk (if you teach more than one class) on the box. When students arrive, familiarize them with the supply boxes. Tell them that they are responsible for checking the box daily and telling the teacher immediately if they notice that anything is missing. This, of course, means that the student in the last class "accidentally" left with something that belongs in the box. The teacher can then retrieve the missing item. The teacher will receive a "reimbursement" of sorts for the cost of the supplies because the students' supply lists include all or most of the items that are in the boxes. As students bring in their supplies, the teacher can collect and stockpile the items as replacements for the remainder of the year. There is usually an amount left over at the end of the year that is sufficient for creating the boxes for the next year.

9. Assign one student per row/group as the materials supervisor and show these students where EVERYTHING lives.

10. Literally determine a space/place for everything. Don't deviate. If an item is taken from its place, it must be returned to its place. No questions asked! No excuses tolerated!

Bottom Line

If we free ourselves of the physical clutter, we free ourselves of the mind clutter. Organization breeds orderliness, and orderliness opens doors to effective teaching and learning. Without organization and order, ultimate teacher effectiveness cannot be reached. An organized environment is a breeding ground for learning.

Within Mr. Laston lies a highly effective, highly knowledgeable teacher, often hidden beneath the disorganization and chaos. He just needs to become organized, and the best teacher that is within him will be free to emerge and grow.

Are you familiar with the "modeling" philosophy, *"They hear what we do?"* Mr. Laston was an excellent model of disorganization. Because of his example, the students in his classroom were disorganized. They exited his room each day leaving it in the same disarray that was there when they arrived. I was able to model for them not only a language arts lesson, but a lesson on organization and efficiency. Do you remember how quickly they conformed? That's one of the beauties of teaching. Students are extremely flexible. They're not nearly as rigid as we teachers are!

The fact is that an organized classroom, because it is free of chaos, runs much more efficiently and effectively. In a teaching environment that has been planned, staged, and organized, the teacher can enjoy the fruits of stress-free teaching. More teaching and learning can occur in less time than in the classroom where precious minutes are robbed by the repercussions of chaos. Which classroom would you choose?

Did You Hear?

Did you hear that Ms. Brown has cautioned and warned
The new teacher in first grade that she will be harmed
If she fails to comply with the rules of her game
And that if she refuses she'll drive her insane?

Did you hear that Ms. Hayes has been snooping around
In the personnel file drawers I heard she was found
And was caught stealing paper and other supplies
From the faculty store room right under our eyes?

Did you hear that the children in Joe's second hour
Are holding the reins and enjoying the power
They're seizing control and they're running the show
And the more that he teaches the less that they know?

Did you hear that our school is at the bottom again
And the school board has no idea where to begin
They're blaming the faculty, parents, and staff
I'd tell them to burn it if only they'd ask.

What did you just tell me, that I am mistaken
I've listened to rumors then peers I've forsaken
I've gossiped to others, I've smeared some good names
I've disgraced the profession and used it for game?

One in which you, of course, would not partake
Regardless of circumstance you'd never make
Buffoons of your peers, your colleagues, and students
You've got too much dignity, self-worth, and prudence.

You say I'd be wise to heed your suggestions
And verify first if the matters in question
Are worth the demise of our school's reputation
Or simply the fruits of my own mind's creation.

—Elizabeth Breaux

Mistake 9:
Being Unprofessional

Defining the Mistake

One of the most dire mistakes a teacher or any other professional can ever make is that of behaving in an unprofessional manner. Behavior that is unethical and childish has no place in our schools. Our purpose as teachers is to assist in the development of the young, those who look to us for guidance, advice, and example. Why, then, would we model for them what we would never deliberately teach?

Unprofessional behavior can be exemplified in hundreds of ways. Most seem to fall under one of the following categories:

♦ Gossiping
♦ Being Negative
♦ Complaining
♦ Practicing Indiscretion
♦ Blaming
♦ Excuse Making

Gossiping

Gossiping is simply a method used to make one feel important. If I know something that you don't know, I have the upper hand, if only for the moment. You need me, which makes me the focal point. It feels good. It's addictive. And it's destructive!

Gossiping may be the number one instigator of fighting among students. We teachers despise it, we preach against it, we admonish those who participate, and then we do it ourselves! Spend too much time in the lounge and you will often depart with far too much information. I caution young teachers today to avoid becoming one of the "lounge lizards." It's quite easy to get sucked in by the "professional" gossipers, and before you know it, you're one of them!

Being Negative

Handling situations in a negative manner is never productive. If a child is speaking out of turn while we are trying to teach, we must avert the behavior. We have a choice in how to accomplish that, however. We can attack the child and the behavior using a destructive approach which will probably escalate the situation, or we can defuse the situation by addressing the behavior, not the child, using a calm, caring, constructive approach. Unstable situations between adults MUST also be coped with using a positive approach.

Negativity has no place in our schools. It's harmful, depressive, and destructive. Words alone can tear down years of building up. Students need positive environments and positive people around them. Far too many of them don't get it at home, but we can and should provide that positive environment for them at school. Negativity encourages more negativity, and before you realize it, it has spread like wildfire. Don't start it, don't engage in it, and don't allow others to draw you into it.

Complaining

The way I see it, I have a choice. I can either spend my days complaining about all of the work required of me, or I can spend my days teaching. There will always be a plethora of issues readily available for me to complain about. Once I've complained about each one, another has been added to the list. Again, it's a choice I make. I can either accept that "it is what it is" and get busy performing the job which I was hired to perform, or I can waste necessary energy complaining about it.

Practicing Indiscretion

Certain issues are inappropriate topics for the classroom. For example, we must keep personal issues separate from issues we must deal with at school. The fact is that we are all human and with that comes an abundance of human-like problems, which should never be brought to school and unloaded on our students. In the "most noble" words of my sister, Annette,

If you do not have personal problems,
then you are not a person.
If you allow your personal problems to spill over into your classroom,
then you are not a professional.

Personal issues that involve other teachers, other students, and so on, are never appropriate topics for whole class discussion. Students will try to engage teachers in such discussions. The professional teachers disapprove of it and would never allow it to take place in their classrooms.

Blaming

The students are academically weak. They seldom turn in homework and are often late for class. We are expected to make them successful, yet we feel slighted and ill-equipped. So what do we do? We engage in the blame game!

- We blame last year's teachers. Had they done their jobs, the students would not be in this predicament.

- We blame their parents. Their lack of support and concern has contributed (if not caused) the situation to be what it is.

- We blame the administration. They should "do something" about these kids before allowing them back into the classrooms. "If I were the principal, I'd whip them into shape!"

- We blame society. Things are not what they used to be.

Then, we find that we are too exhausted to teach. We have given ourselves every reason to fail. We have written students their own tickets for failure. We have removed the possibilities.

Excuse-Making

We seem to have excuses for everything. We have excuses for not turning in lesson plans. We have excuses for being late for faculty meetings. We have excuses for failing to report to our duty stations in timely fashion. We have excuses for not turning in important paperwork on time. *Yet we detest and are intolerant of excuse-making from our students!*

Examples of the Mistake

Let's face it: life happens! Children get sick, the car has a flat tire, there's a wreck on the freeway. We've got doctors' appointments and little league ball games. One or more of these has been an issue for every one of us, so we all understand and expect the unexpected to happen, especially when we least expect or can least afford for it to happen!

Mrs. Vahn was the exception. Several of these things happened to her, every day, for as long as the administration and teachers could remember. Mrs. Vahn was usually late for school. Neighboring teachers were often asked to watch her first period class until she arrived. She always seemed frazzled, running around in bizarre fashion in search of this or that. The bell to indicate the beginning of first period rang at 7:30, and Mrs. Vahn always raced into the building somewhere between 7:30 and 7:35. (Teachers were required to arrive at 7:15.) This went on for several years. She always had an excuse. The pages of a book could have been filled with the excuses she gathered over the years.

Then one year the school system decided to change the starting and ending times of the school day. The usual 7:30 commencement time was changed to 8:00. The teachers who were often affected by Mrs. Vahn's tardiness were thrilled and relieved. No longer would they be forced to bear the brunt of Mrs. Vahn's unprofessional behavior. Surely this habitual tardiness would occur no more. Not so. Can you guess at what time she began arriving? You guessed it: somewhere between 8:00 and 8:05.

It probably goes without saying, but I'll mention it anyway. Mrs. Vahn was usually late for or absent from important meetings. She was often late to arrive to her duty station. She did have excuses, however, and seemed to actually believe that they were valid. Is this behavior reminiscent of some of your students' behaviors?

Mr. Siegen complains about everything. The books are too old. The children are disrespectful. The administration is too lenient. The teachers are too accommodating. The school board expects too much. Attending after-school meetings is not in his contract. He doesn't have enough computers in his room. The paperwork is overwhelming. The curriculum is ridiculous. And on and on and on.

He also complains that his "requests" are rarely taken seriously. He's probably correct in that assumption. His incessant complaining has manifested itself in such a way that others no longer take him seriously. His negativity toward everyone has forced others around him to create barriers for their own protection. Just being in the same room with him is unpleasant. Fortunately for the teachers, they have the option of excusing themselves from his presence. His students are not afforded that option!

Correcting the Mistake

Unprofessional behaviors practiced by those who claim to be professionals must be addressed and rectified. My hope for you is that you and your fellow teachers are supported by a strong, caring administration, one that will not tolerate unprofessional behavior on any level.

If you fear that you have acted in an unprofessional manor, rectify it. Acknowledge it and make necessary amends. Model the behaviors that you would like for your students to acquire.

If you ever find yourself pondering whether or not you have acted unprofessionally in a given situation, pause and imagine someone else committing that same act. Did it seem unprofessional when performed by another? That's your answer.

Avoiding the Mistake

Young teachers, especially, get sucked in by the negative, complaining, blaming, and excuse-making of others who are in relentless search of new members to join their teams. These veterans feed on the young, inexperienced teachers, those who are yearning to be part of the group. Don't conform. Once they see you as the consummate professional that you are, they'll relent.

Avoid negative people as much as possible. The complaining, blaming, and excuse-making is contagious and can be contracted when least expected. Once you're inflicted, recovery is difficult.

Bottom Line

As professionals, we must behave professionally at all times. Like it or not, the students are watching. We cannot model for them what we would never intentionally teach them. The fact is that they hear what we do much more loudly than they hear what we say. Unprofessional behaviors affect everyone and, if allowed to continue, become insidious. There is no place for them on our campuses. Students are exposed to enough unprofessional behaviors in today's world. Be a model of professionalism at all times and at all costs. It, too, is contagious!

If I can just remember that my words are simply sounds
That children hear in one ear and out, too often I have found
And more compared to what I do (or less to be exact),
For what I do is what they hear, this matter is a fact
Children watch our every move, it's what we "do," not "say"
That they will mimic every time, the powers in the play.

—Elizabeth Breaux
From *How to Reach and Teach ALL Students—Simplified*

My Legacy

If I could leave one legacy to all of those I've taught
I'd wish that aspirations, faith and dreams were what I'd wrought
I'd like to know I'd left them all with yearnings and desires
And hungry souls that burn in them like raging, blazing fires.

I'd want them all to know there is no mountain they can't climb
No river that they cannot ford, no quandary they can't rhyme
No expectations they can't meet, no prospects ever bleak
No shining star, no rainbow's end, no dream they cannot seek.

No likelihood of failure if it's not for lack of trying
No reward that's worth its salt if someone else is buying,
No end to ever questioning the marvels of this world
This legacy I'd leave to you, my precious boys and girls.

—Elizabeth Breaux

Mistake 10:
Lowering Expectations

Defining the Mistake

A 6-year-old child once said, *"My teacher thought I was much smarter than I was, so I was."* A more profound yet unpretentiously direct and accurate statement I have never heard. Those much older and wiser could not have articulated it more perfectly.

Children believe what they are told. They internalize our opinions and expectations of them. They will become whatever we truly believe that they are capable of becoming. They will accomplish whatever those around them feel they are capable of accomplishing. We have the power to stifle their potential, or to assist them in reaching and ultimately exceeding the possibilities.

Having taught and worked with at-risk students for 24 years, I can confirm without reservation that most of them have seldom, if ever, achieved what they are capable of accomplishing. Most of them, sadly, believe that they are not capable. Why? It happens because the teachers and other adults in their lives believe that they are incapable of accomplishing more. As a result, they, the students, seem "comfortable" being where they are.

If you believe that you cannot achieve, you will not. If I, your teacher, believe that you cannot achieve, I have confirmed your belief in yourself. The bar has been set, much too low. Surpassing it will never happen, because no one remotely expects that it will. Without positive expectations, there can be no goals. Without goals, there is no striving. Without striving, there is stagnation, often followed by regression.

Example of the Mistake

Most students will accomplish no more than is required. Teachers who expect little usually require little and accept less. Mrs. Mason is one of those teachers.

Mrs. Mason teaches math at an at-risk school. The school is considered "one in decline," a rating given to it because of extremely low school performance scores. Mrs. Mason has taught at this school for over 20 years. This year is no different from any other. According to Mrs. Mason:

- ◆ The students are extremely weak.
- ◆ The students' computational skills are severely lacking.
- ◆ The students don't care.
- ◆ The students are unmotivated.
- ◆ The parents don't care.

- The administration is unsupportive.
- Most of the students are going to fail.

Her preconceived notions do not waver as time progresses. Her expectations are low, sometimes nonexistent. She expects no more than she believes that the students are capable of accomplishing. Since she believes that they are basically incapable of accomplishing much, her expectations are minimal. Her "lessons" are driven by her beliefs.

I walked into her classroom one day for an informal observation. I sat in the back and began observing. This eighth-grade math class was completing basic multiplication and division problems, while she sat at her desk. Once the students completed their worksheets, the lesson proceeded. She provided the correct answer to each problem. Some students corrected their incorrect responses; some did not bother to do so. There was no explaining or reteaching involved. Most students were inattentive.

It was December, and the state test was to be given in March. I'm no expert in math, but I knew that on the state test students were required to apply the basic skills at higher levels, levels where they must analyze using critical-thinking skills. They must be able to decipher word problems and determine steps necessary to solve those problems. Once that process is determined, the basic computational skills are applied. My concern was that this class seemed to be stuck on the basics, and I wondered how they would ever arrive at the level necessary to achieve on the test.

My suspicions were confirmed when I spoke to Mr. Charles, the chairperson of the math department.

"Mrs. Mason refuses to challenge her students," he said. "Her belief in their abilities is nil. Her negative attitude and demeanor are striking evidence of those beliefs. She has no confidence in the students. For that reason, the students have no confidence in themselves. I've attempted to assist her by sharing some new strategies and ideas, but she has rejected the help. I am afraid that her classes are destined for failure again this year."

Mr. Charles went on to suggest that I observe the other eighth-grade class.

"You should observe Mrs. Andrews, another eighth-grade math teacher here. You wouldn't believe what she is able to accomplish with her students. And by the way, and in case you didn't already know, Mrs. Andrews' students are the weakest in the school. They are considered the 'below average' class. They don't seem to know that, however. Mrs. Andrews has them believing that they can outscore anyone!"

Fixing the Mistake

I entered Mrs. Andrews' room and sat in the back to observe. The first thing I noticed was that the students seemed much older than those in Mrs. Mason's class. I learned later that Mrs. Andrews' students, although eighth graders, were all at least a year or two behind in grade level. As I recalled from my conversation with Mr. Charles, this was considered the "below average" class. You'd never believe it if you didn't already know it!

Mrs. Andrews was everywhere, scurrying around from one student to another. All students were on task and working diligently. Mrs. Andrews was "high-fiving" and "good-jobbing" as she scuttled from student to student. I noticed what seemed to be a relatively difficult word problem on the white board in front of the class. Notations were made, lines were drawn, and references were indicated in different colors, which made them easy to understand. Mrs. Andrews would intermittently run back to the board, explain another part of the sequence, draw some more lines and arrows, question the students; and then everyone would get back to the task at hand: trying to solve the problem. Once all had finished, Mrs. Andrews returned to the front of the room. She grilled the students on every aspect of the process, refusing to accept correct answers without viable, reasonable explanations. Mrs. Andrews praised every correct response, commended every effort, and applauded every success.

Mr. Charles had been right. Had I not known better, I would have thought that this was an advanced class, instead of one considered below average. The bar had been raised in this class. That was obvious.

After class ended, I stayed to talk to Mrs. Andrews and to applaud her efforts and accomplishments. She admitted to me that when the students had come to her they were very academically weak, and most were unable to complete basic multiplication and division problems.

"I don't have the time to stay stuck on that," she said. "There are much bigger fish to fry."

I inquired as to how she had gotten them to this level.

"We just get right in there and do it," she said. "Initially we do a little drill and practice session involving basic skills at the beginning of each class. It's very intense, but they pick it up fairly quickly. Then, I place a calculator in their hands! Like I said, those 'bigger fish' are waiting out there for us, and we don't have time to waste. These children are quite capable. They just don't know it at first. Once they taste success, there is no stopping them!"

I couldn't imagine anyone stopping Mrs. Andrews either!

Avoiding the Mistake

First, a word of caution: We *must* keep expectations high, but we *must never* expect too much too soon! A correct balance of both is critical. In chapter 4 we discussed the importance of making students successful, at their own levels, before challenging them to perform at higher levels. Success breeds success. A small taste is often the impetus that leads to the quest for more.

On one hand, Mrs. Andrews had very high expectations for her students. On the other, she knew better than to expect too much too soon. By maintaining high expectations, she did not allow her students to remain stagnant, because they were constantly being challenged at progressively higher levels. By maintaining a system where achievements were progressive, one building upon the other, she made sure the students were never discouraged, as would have happened had too much been expected of them too soon.

In order to avoid the mistake of lowering expectations, we must be aware of where our students are academically and in what direction we plan to lead them.

Bottom Line

Students will have only as much faith in themselves as we, their teachers, have in them. We must raise the bar and then convince them that they are capable of surmounting it. The only way to do that is to make them successful. Since success is built upon other successes, teachers must strive to make their students successful. Only then can we challenge them to perform at higher levels.

Too much potential is left untapped. Too few students ever exceed that of which they are capable. We, the teachers, can rectify that. We must believe so that we can help them achieve. Believe in your students, and they will believe in themselves.

All Is Fair

When all is fair in love and war where anything suffices
The rules and regulations are left to our own devices
At times we must consider different sets of circumstances
"That for them" and "these for those" so everyone advances.

When playing fields are level and everything's the same
The rules pertain to everyone partaking in the game
But when the turfs are not alike, all players don't compare
And "all for one" and "one for all" is not exactly fair.

Sometimes being "fair" and "just" means treating all the same
Conversely, treating "same as" can disqualify the game
When special situations call for singular creations
Do what's best for each and thus avoid the confrontations.

—Elizabeth Breaux

Mistake 11:
Treating Students Unfairly

Defining the Mistake

In certain situations, being fair requires that all are treated the same. It ensures that all adhere to the same rules and regulations. Failure to follow the rules results in a consequence or penalty, one that is the same for each infraction, regardless of the player. For the most part, those committing infractions are treated equally, which means that they are treated fairly.

In other situations, fair play requires that players are treated differently.

♦ Would a blind child be asked to recite poetry from the chalkboard?

♦ Would a child with a broken foot be expected to run a mile?

♦ Would all patients be given the same medication, regardless of illness?

Generally speaking, rules are meant to be followed by everyone. This is the only way to ensure order and control environments. Classroom rules and procedures help to ensure effective management and provide an appropriate learning environment. In most situations, it is critical that all adhere to the same rules, and that all are justly punished, in an equitable manner, when those rules are broken.

Conversely, it's critical to understand that treating students fairly does not always mean treating all students exactly the same. In some situations fairness means treating the student in a manner that can evoke the best results from that particular student. That method may be entirely different from one that would generate the best results from another student. In a situation such as this, being fair means treating students differently.

Contrary to the old saying, "rules are made to be broken," rules are actually made with the intent that everyone will be expected to follow them. Every municipality, business, home, school, and so on, must maintain order. Without it, chaos will be its downfall. Schools are simply extensions of the real world. Without order, they cannot survive and thrive.

Examples of the Mistake

Ms. Rogers teaches 25 exuberant, energetic, and high-spirited third graders. As is the case in any class, a few are a bit more exuberant and high-spirited than the others. Jeremy, especially, can't seem to sit still for more than a few minutes at a time before becoming restless and fidgety. In order to tend to Jeremy's needs, the teacher often has her attention directed toward him and away from the other students. Ms. Rogers has noticed that disciplining Jeremy in front of the others often makes matters worse. Since allowing this behavior to continue would not be an option (because it would not be fair to the other students), Ms. Rogers needs to be creative in devising a fair way to address and remedy this situation.

Ms. Rogers creates a "special" area of the room just for Jeremy. She creates a circle about 4 feet in diameter. She places an extra desk within the circle. She shows Jeremy his special place. She tells him that whenever he feels the need to stand or move around, he may move to this area. He must, however, bring his work with him. He may not talk to or disturb others along the way. Once in his area, he may sit or stand to do his work, as long as he stays within the confines of the area. As long as he behaves and complies with the rules, he can use this area.

The next day, when Jeremy began to squirm in his desk, Ms. Rogers simply pointed to the circle. She moved closely to Jeremy and led him to the circle. She continued teaching so as not to allow this to become the focus of the class. Once Jeremy was clearly within the confines of the area, she whispered to him a reminder: "Don't forget to stay inside of the circle. You can sit or stand, but you must continue working just like the rest of the class." Ms. Rogers kept her eye on him on that first occasion. After that, Jeremy seldom needed her assistance.

The other students did not feel as though they were being treated unfairly. They actually appreciated the fact that Ms. Rogers had created this special place for Jeremy. By doing so, Ms. Rogers was able to focus more of her attention on the other students. Thus, Ms. Rogers had to treat Jeremy differently so that she could be fair to everyone else.

Now let's look at Arcadia Middle School's tardy policy as a prime example of the reason rules are necessary. At AMS students are allowed 3 minutes between class periods to go from one room to the next. The school's policy is that all students must be inside the doors of the rooms when the tardy bell sounds. Failure to do so results in one recorded tardy for that particular class. The rule includes the following consequences:

1. First Tardy: Warning and recorded in teacher's log
2. Second Tardy: Recorded in teacher's log. Parents notified.
3. Third Tardy: Office referral (in-school suspension).
4. Fourth Tardy: Office referral (Saturday school).
5. Fifth Tardy: Office referral (out- of-school suspension).
6. Sixth Tardy: Office referral (out-of- school suspension).
7. Seventh Tardy: Office Referral (recommended expulsion).

Teachers in the school are all required to adhere to the policy. A visitor in the school would notice that when the tardy bell rings, there are seldom any students in the hallways. This had not been the case before the implementation of the policy.

As is the case in any school, a number of students will test any rule so as to determine if it's "for real." Some students at AMS have learned the hard way that it is no fallacy. Several have spent time in the in-school suspension program. A few have spent time at school on Saturdays. A couple of students have received out-of-school suspensions. None have ever reached the point of expulsion.

One of Mr. Dixon's students is a victim of a recent car accident. He has a broken leg and is walking on crutches. Should the rule still apply to him? Of course not. I don't think anyone would argue with that. Teachers have made the necessary accommodations for him. They either allow him to leave class early or they excuse his late arrivals. Do the other students think that this is unfair? Of course not. Everyone would agree that the tardy policy, in its current state, must be amended for such a situation as this.

Mr. Simon teaches reading to 10 students with disabilities. All have specific, individual accommodation plans. Three of his students are hearing impaired. Two of them are visually impaired. The rest have mild learning disabilities resulting from a variety of reasons. Will all of these students be taught the same materials, at the same time, using the same approach? Will all be taught at the same pace? Will all be tested using the same assessment procedures? Hopefully not. That would be a huge mistake. It simply would not be fair to the students. In this case, being "fair" requires that students are treated "differently."

Correcting the Mistake

In all of the previous scenarios, teachers made the necessary accommodations. The mistake of treating all students the same would have resulted in unfair treatment of those who required special considerations. When teachers accommodated individual needs, some students were treated differently from others. However all students were treated fairly.

Avoiding the Mistake

Treating students unfairly must be avoided at all costs. When students feel slighted, especially by an adult in whose care they are placed, trust issues inevitably evolve. When trusts are broken, defenses become inflated. When defenses are raised, barriers are built. The result is an environment that is no longer conducive to learning.

Tips for Treating Students Fairly

- Remember that "fair" does not always mean "the same as."
- Sometimes, being fair to all means treating some differently from the others.
- Except with extreme exceptions (as in the case of the young man with the broken foot), rules are made to be followed.
- Teachers must implement rules, regulations, and policies with utter consistency. If it's policy, follow it as dictated.
- It is never fair to neglect making accommodations that are necessary for the good of the individual. One of our greatest mistakes as teachers is thinking that everyone is the same.

Bottom Line

Treating students fairly does not mean treating them all the same. In fact, in many instances, it means quite the opposite. I have never known a fair teacher to be ineffective or an unfair teacher to be effective. It all boils down to matters of trust. When students trust you to handle situations fairly, they will perform for you because they believe in you. When a mutual respect is nurtured, one where the environment is safe, a learning atmosphere conducive to learning is evident.

Teachers who treat students fairly, who implement procedures with consistency, and who enforce classroom rules uniformly are admired, respected, and trusted by their students. That does not always mean that the child is perfectly happy with the outcome of the situation. But it does mean that the child understands and expects the outcome as a fair and just consequence. Show me a teacher who treats students with consistency, dignity, respect, and fairness, and I'll show you a successful teacher with a classroom full of successful students. Fair enough?

These urgencies are killing me, impeding my best teaching
The "criticals" and "vitals" are keeping me from reaching
The students whom I once thought were entrusted to my care
(I'm biting all my fingernails and pulling out my hair).

I'm checking pressing matters that are written on my list
I'm flashing through each one so fast it's barely hit and miss
But dare that I neglect a few and I'm inviting trouble
So I'll rush through each one of them and do it on the double.

Those of high priority might fail to make the listing
When those of insignificance are very rarely missing
Just because it's urgent doesn't make it influential
And inclusion on the list does not ensure it has potential.

So take your rigid lists away and give me back my slate
And let me place important things back on my teacher's plate
Forget about your timelines with its due dates and its rules
And let me be the teacher we had when we were in school.

—Elizabeth Breaux

Mistake 12:
Neglecting Priorities

Defining the Mistake

The fact is that teachers must prioritize. Neglecting to complete certain tasks and to meet critical deadlines is simply not optional. If something is a priority, it's of utmost importance. It cannot be neglected.

We must become masters at juggling all of the day-to-day responsibilities that we assume as teachers. We must plan well, prepare our rooms properly, teach the prescribed material within the prescribed frame of time, attend meetings, conduct parent conferences, complete paperwork, monitor duty stations, and so on.

Because we get so consumed by the day-to-day urgencies, we often tend to neglect those matters that are of equal importance, yet do not seem at the time to be quite as urgent.

- We neglect to deviate from the planned lesson when a teachable moment occurs, because we are pressed by time to complete it and move forward.
- We fail to make the real-life connection to subject matter when time constraints, again, do not appear to allow for it.
- We remove critical subject matter, that which teaches lifelong lessons, if it is not included on the "test."
- We teach the "text" in lieu of the students.
- We neglect ourselves and become so overwhelmed that our students often get only that part of us that is left over, which is not sufficient.
- We prioritize according to urgencies instead of necessities, and we often forget the difference between the two.

This often carries into, and sometimes originates in, our home lives as well.

- How often have you regretted missing an event or special occasion as a result of its not having been high enough on your "list?"
- How often have you completely missed today while planning for tomorrow?
- When was the last time you said "No" to someone because you didn't have the time?
- When was the last time you said "Yes" to something that was not planned?

It has often been said that, *"The things we will regret the most are those that we have not done."*

Example of the Mistake

First, let me admit that I am the perpetual "list maker." I make a list and then I commence its undertaking. I am not content until all items on my list have been completed. I am uncomfortable if something causes me to deviate from my list, even if that something is of great value to me now or somewhere down the road. I would prefer to remove an item from my list as opposed to allowing it to remain unattended. I have a problem, and I probably need help!

My good friend, Laurie, is completely opposite. She never makes a list! She is one of those people who will do anything for anyone. Just ask and she will be happy to accommodate. The problem is that she fails to write down what she has agreed to do and often forgets to do it! She has a problem, and she definitely needs help! (I know I could help her if she'd just listen to my advice!)

The truth is that there is a much more sensible (and much saner) middle ground where Laurie and I should probably meet. (I'll meet her there as soon as I've accomplished everything on today's list, but she'll never arrive since she'll have neglected to write it down.)

I am a prime example of how this mistake carries over into the classroom, given that my teaching career has taken me through the two generations of teaching: *"Before Testing"* and *"After Testing!"*

In the Before-Testing days (I am referring to both state and national testing of our students, using both norm and criterion-referenced tests), teaching seemed more flexible. Of course we planned our lessons, usually in alignment with the text (if we were fortunate enough to own one), but we were not so unyielding in regard to deviating from the plan. We welcomed spontaneous teachable moments. We gave much less credence to the clock. Even I, the consummate planner, actually planned for (allotted time for) those enlightening moments. I cherished them and understood that the very fact that they could not be planned was what afforded them such quality. I believe that some of the best teaching that occurred in my classroom back then was completely impromptu, yet of utter importance, in spite of its not having been included on my "list!" In retrospect, I realize that some of the most important, critical moments, those that served as such necessary stepping stones for my future and for the futures of my students, had not been preconceived or viewed as being critical at all.

Several years into my teaching career came the dawn of the "testing" age. Life in the classroom seemed to revolve around one test. After-Testing classrooms took on a new demeanor. They became much less spontaneous. The beauty of the naturally evolving classroom saw its demise. The After-Testing classrooms were unyielding and often quite inflexible. Teachers, many of us, became more edgy and anxious. It was not of our own making. We simply had too much to do in too little time and we panicked!

Fortunately for all teachers and our students, we have attained that "happy medium" in this world of testing. We've learned through trial and error that we can teach the necessities while still teaching the human beings: our students. We've come to realize and accept that for the most part these tests are but extensions of our classrooms. They are in most instances relatable to real-life. We know now that we can still teach the material, in a real-life format, while successfully preparing our students. We can still address what is important in the content of the lesson and include what is not as critical but is of equal importance.

Correcting the Mistake

Are you forgetful? We all are. We all need a little help from time to time in remembering to complete those things that are crucial. Lists are meant to be used as guides and reminders. With all that is expected of teachers today, we need all the help we can get. With all of the deadlines and timelines in today's world of teaching, we cannot simply rely on our memory. We need extra assistance. Certain duties must be completed within time restraints, like it or not. If it's due next Friday, write it on next Friday's calendar. If you commit to something, commit to not neglecting it. Others are counting on you.

Do you struggle with trying to determine which items are of highest priority? Do you already prioritize, but still neglect some of the priorities? If you do, ask yourself this:

What is it that, at the end of the day (or the end of my life), I will regret most?

Whatever your answer, check your list. Is it there?

Avoiding the Mistake

If we choose wisely, we can avoid the mistake of neglecting priorities. We must commit to doing whatever it takes to avoid overlooking important everyday obligations. Here are a few tips that will help to keep you on track:

♦ Keep an updated calendar that is available to you at all times.

♦ Write important due dates down immediately. A calendar is of no use if you neglect to use it. Requirements that have deadlines are not optional. Complete them by (or before) the deadline.

♦ Plan for the unexpected. Life happens. Don't let it catch you off-guard.

♦ Include the really important (but not crucial at the moment) items on your list. Those are the ones you will regret neglecting.

♦ Lesson plans should be guides. Know that they are subject to change at a moment's notice. The most teachable moments (crucial ones that may not have been given priority) are the ones that cannot be planned.

♦ Lesson plans must contain the "must do's." If you can't get to it today, you "must do" it tomorrow.

♦ Consider your actions, or lack thereof, and how they will impact others. Will your failure to act have the domino effect? For example, will failure to do your part upset the whole?

Bottom Line

The most effective, respected, and influential teachers are those who maintain the delicate balance between tasks which are urgent and must be attended to and tasks which are not as urgent, yet still of high priority. They are the teachers who are able to meet all of the mandated requirements, while still maintaining their ability to be spontaneous when delivering a planned lesson. They are the teachers who recognize that important matters, those with lifelong implications, are sometimes neglected because the urgency is not as apparent.

The best teachers are those who make things happen and who allow things to naturally evolve. They look at the big picture, one that doesn't always appear clear at the moment, but that requires foresight. They are the ones who won't get bogged down in those things that are simply not important and have no foreseeable relevance. These teachers are not time wasters, but in fact are very efficient time managers. They must be! How else could they get so much done, while never appearing to be stressed out or overworked?

Take a look at your list of priorities. You may want to reprioritize some of it!

Which Is It?

There is a poster on the wall, it lists our classroom rules
And I'm supposed to follow them as long as I'm in school
Raise your hand, do your work, be timely and prepared
Complete your homework on your own, do not attempt to share
Stay in your seat and off your feet unless you ask permission
Don't think you're going anywhere, if that's what you were wishin'.

I wonder why that poster is there, since no one seems to use it
If nothing else I'd have to say that we have all abused it
We talk out loud, we walk around, and mostly never listen
We even leave the room and very seldom ask permission
Some days our teacher doesn't mind, on others she's demanding
Yelling, screaming, punishing, all sorts of reprimanding.

It's really quite confusing since we never can rely
On knowing whether this might be the day when they apply
Yesterday they didn't, but the day before they did
That's the day she was so mad she nearly flipped her lid
She punished Stanley Stonewall, and threatened Mandy Munn
All and all I must admit that day was really fun!

—Elizabeth Breaux

Mistake 13:
Being Inconsistent

Defining the Mistake

Teachers covet an administration that is structured, dependable, and enthusiastic. We appreciate a leader who maintains harmony by treating all with fairness and impartiality. We welcome the leader who will be consistent, across the board, when implementing the rules and procedures that will help our school to run smoothly and efficiently.

So why is it, then, that we often neglect or forget to manage those under our leadership using that same approach? In my opinion, based on my experiences while observing countless teachers, one of the biggest deterrents to effective teaching and learning in our classrooms is the lack of consistencies in our dealings with children. The greatest obstacle to classroom management is not the students, although they are usually the first at whom the finger is pointed. Remember that they are children whether they are 5 years old or 18 years old! We are the adults.

Children, like adults, yearn for a structured environment. They crave and need dependable, trustworthy leadership. Such an environment cannot be built in the midst of inconsistencies.

Classroom rules are imposed so that order can be maintained. They are usually posted in an area of the room where they can be easily seen by everyone. Rarely have I entered a classroom where rules were not posted in a highly visible area of the room. It seems that rules are typically somewhat generic, in spite of grade or age level. The more common ones include:

- Raise your hand to speak.
- Keep your hands to yourself.
- Be on time.
- Bring your materials to class.
- Ask permission to leave your desk.
- Respect others.
- Pick up trash.

If this list of rules is fairly typical of what is required in most classrooms, why is it that every single one of those classrooms is not running efficiently? And why is it that some of them are actually functioning beautifully? It depends on whether or not the leader, the teacher, is utterly consistent in the implementation. The teacher is the bottom line. If the teachers fail to be consistent in the implementation of rules and procedures, the students will show inconsistencies in following the rules and procedures. One is a direct effect of the other.

Let's make a clear distinction between a *rule* and a *procedure*.

- A *rule* has a consequence attached to it. Students must receive a punishment or consequence of some sort if a rule is broken.

- A *procedure* is a day-to-day classroom function that makes the lesson run smoothly. There is no need to implement a consequence or a punishment if a procedure is not performed correctly, because there is no violation of a rule. *EXCEPTION: A child who willfully refuses to follow a procedure after adequate practice time may need a consequence. Before doing so, however, exhaust all other possibilities, such as calling the parent or having a one-on-one conversation with the student.*

The well managed classroom will have many procedures and just a few rules. If the teacher implements the procedures effectively, many of what we used to consider rules can become procedures. Some expectations *must* take the form of a rule, however. Hitting, tardiness, and disrespect, for example, are infractions that must be dealt with by implementing a very definitive consequence, immediately and consistently.

In reference to classroom rules, the teacher must explain the expectation in a precise manner and explain the consequence that follows the infraction. (Consequences should be visually indicated next to each rule.)

In reference to classroom procedures, the teacher must go through the following three steps before they can become routines:

1. Teach
2. Practice
3. Implement

In step one, the *teaching* step, the teacher must literally teach the students the exact method in which a particular procedure is to take place. Tell them, show them, and then tell them again and show them again!

In step two, the *practicing* step, the teacher must allow the students to actually try it themselves. This can be great fun and a wonderful learning experience. Tell your students that this is the time to mess up! In fact, encourage them to make mistakes. Tell them it's okay to make mistakes in order to learn the proper way.

In step three, the *implementation* step, the teacher begins *consistent* implementation of what has been taught and practiced! If a child performs the procedure incorrectly, the teacher simply reminds him/her of the correct procedure, immediately, and then has the student practice it until it becomes routine.

Examples of the Mistake

The procedure for *getting the teacher's attention* has been taught and practiced. Students have been taught that they must raise their hands to speak … period … at all times. An observer notices that one student blurts out a question. In response, the teacher answers the question. This happens several times. Once it has become flagrant and disruptive, the teacher tells the students that they are supposed to raise their hands before speaking.

The school policy states that all students must be in the classroom when the tardy bell rings. Doors must then be closed. An observer standing in the hallway notices that several students trickle into one classroom several minutes late every day. It's glaring because all other doors in that hallway are closed when the tardy bell rings.

The procedure for *leaving one's desk* has been taught and practiced. Students have been taught that they must ask permission to leave their desks … period … at all times. An observer notices that students are walking to the garbage can at will. One student has left his desk, without permission, to sharpen his pencil. Another student proceeds to the front of the room, while the teacher is teaching, to ask a question of the teacher. The teacher answers the question then continues teaching. Finally, when another student attempts to make her way to the front of the room to ask a question, the teacher stops her. The student becomes angry, grumbling words of disgust as she makes her way back to her seat.

Correcting the Mistake

The procedure for getting the teacher's attention had been taught and practiced. The breakdown came in the implementation phase, where the teacher allowed incorrect implementation to occur in several separate instances. The teacher allowed several students to blurt out questions before attempting to rectify the mistakes. Had the teacher immediately reminded the first child by having him/her stop, raise their hand, and then ask the question, other students might not have made the attempts. The teacher must set the precedent, immediately, or the mistake will continue until it snowballs into something that is far more difficult to manage.

A deeper look into the classroom where students arrive late every day would quickly reveal the problem. The teacher "fusses" but never records the offenses. Consequences are in place but not implemented with consistency. Students know that nothing will happen to them, so they continue to arrive late. A look into some of the other classrooms in the same hallway would reveal quite the opposite. The teachers have been meticulous about recording offenses and following through with the consequences. As a result, students no longer arrive late to those classes.

The procedure for leaving your desk has been taught and practiced. The implementation phase, however, was not performed with consistency. The teacher allowed several students to leave their desks without permission before attempting to implement the procedure as it had been taught and practiced. The result was a frustrated teacher and one very angry young girl. The teacher should have stopped the behavior the very first time it happened. Failure to do so caused the students to doubt their teacher. The result was that they continued their attempts to "change" the procedure to suit their own whims, as all students (people) will do if the leadership is weak and inconsistent.

Avoiding the Mistake

In order to avoid the need to fix the mistake, take a proactive approach from the very first day of school. First, determine which expectations will become rules and which will become procedures. Make a list of each and be ready to present each to your class on the very first day(s) of school. Following are examples of my own lists of rules and procedures. The procedures list is simply a sample, since through the years most expectations become procedural and the result is that there are many procedures and few rules.

Rules

1. Be on time.
2. Respect others.
3. Maintain your composure.
4. Submit work on time.
5. Bring materials.

Procedures

Here are just a few of them, which can all be found in more detail in my book *Classroom Management Simplified 2* (2005).

- Taking the Roll
- Sharpening Pencils
- Getting the Students' Attention
- Talking in Class
- Using Classroom Materials and Supplies
- Distributing and Collecting Materials
- Managing Group-work
- Discarding Trash
- Calling Home
- Requesting Water and Bathroom Privileges
- Taking a Test
- Attending Assemblies
- … and MANY more!

Bottom Line

It is the sole responsibility of the teacher to determine rules and procedures, except for the few that will be dictated by the school board and/or administration, in his/her classroom. If the teacher does not determine the rules and procedures in the classroom, the students will do it. They will begin in the first minutes of the first day of school. If this is allowed, it will escalate. No doubt about it. Once that happens, it is much more difficult to fix. In order to avoid the mistake, we must become proactive in our approach.

- Be assertive and decisive.
- Spend some time *Teaching* the procedures and rules.
- Spend some time *Practicing* the procedure. (Don't forget to actually encourage mistakes during this step.)
- Begin consistent *Implementation* of the procedure and rules immediately.
- Correct any improper implementation immediately. Failure to do so is a sure recipe for failure.

I've known since I was little that a teacher I'd become
Every chance I'd get I would pretend that I was one
I'd contact all the children living up and down the street
Instructing them that at my house is where we all would meet.

I'd sharpen every pencil, I'd straighten every row
I'd meet the kids in our front yard then off to "school" we'd go
I'd line them up in single file from little ones to tall
Then spout each name out from the role that I'd proceed to call.

I'd tell them stories and pretend that they were really true
What's the harm, I'd ask myself, if no one ever knew?
I've got to be creative if to garner their attention
The fact that it's a lie is something I'll forget to mention.

I'd grill them on their words and rhymes their multiples and fractions
I'd place a star upon their tests and relish their reactions
I'd punish each and every one who would attempt to chatter
And send them to the corner which would rectify the matter.

I'd check completed papers; I'd hand out all the snacks
I'd even put the little ones all down to have their naps
I'd thank them all for coming, and I'd send them on their way
And lie there in exhaustion from my quite eventful day!

Then I'd get back to planning for my next exciting lesson
It had to be a good one or they wouldn't come I'm guessing
I'd summon my creative side to aid origination
After all it was, for them, their summertime vacation!

—Elizabeth Breaux

Mistake 14: Planning Haphazardly

Defining the Mistake

What is the cost of success and how much are you willing to pay? The answer to those questions is what distinguishes the great teachers from all of the rest. Are you willing to pay a price that may be much higher than the one for which you originally bargained? In case you didn't know, the price is always much higher than the price you thought you'd pay.

Teaching is not for the faint of heart. It is not for the lazy. It is not for the weak, the weary, or the meek! Teaching is hard work, often much harder than ever imagined. Are you up for the task?

Don't be fooled by what teaching looks like. To the untrained person, teachers have it made!

- They are off at 3:00 every day.
- They don't work on weekends.
- They only work for half of the year.
- They are off all summer.
- They get 4 to 5 weeks per year of paid vacation.

If you are laughing, then you are a teacher! If you're not a teacher, and are planning to become one, you are in for a huge, mind-boggling, earth shattering, inconceivable surprise!

- The 3:00 bell indicates *student* dismissal. Some teachers are just beginning their work day!
- Weekends are some of our busiest planning days. Without them, we'd be ill-prepared for the coming week.
- We may teach for "only" 180 days or so per year, but the rest is spent planning for teaching.
- Off during the summer? Are you kidding? We've got another year to plan, a room to be made ready, workshops to attend, new materials to study, a changing curriculum to master, and so on.
- The paid vacations are not as they seem. We may receive a check, but it's money we've already earned that the board hasn't given to us yet!

The great teachers have learned that their busiest times are those spent planning. Effective lessons don't create themselves. Even if they did, as in the case of having someone else plan a lesson for you, the teacher is the one responsible for effectively implementing that lesson. The same lesson implemented by two different teachers can have drastically different outcomes.

Failing to plan is a plan for failure. Even the best teachers are at their best only once proper planning has occurred. None of us are ever as effective when we ad-lib as we are when we teach a lesson that is well-prepared and thought out. An ill-planned lesson yields ill-equipped students.

Is it possible to fake your way through a poorly prepared lesson? Possibly, if you're good actors and actresses. Will students suffer in the long run? Absolutely. Every time. Without fail. Our schools are filled with both real teachers and imposters. Which one will you be?

Example of the Mistake

The mistake comes in not realizing that effective planning is the key to the effective implementation of anything. Imagine taking your family on a vacation that was not planned? The thought of doing that is absurd. We know better. Imagine leaving with no knowledge of where you were headed. You'd have no roadmap for the trip. No hotel reservations. No money. No clothes. Ridiculous! In the same manner:

- ♦ Would you attempt to take your students on a field trip without thoroughly and comprehensively planning every detail?
- ♦ Would you fail to plan for an announced observation by a supervisor from the central office or school board?
- ♦ Would you attempt to teach a daily lesson without having planned with attention to all details? Unfortunately, many do. This mistake is unconscionable and unacceptable, yet I've seen it happen over and over again.

Correcting the Mistake

First, acknowledge whether or not you are guilty of having made the mistake. Most of us have had days when we were not as well prepared as we should have been. Why was that?

- ♦ Had I simply chosen to make the mistake?
- ♦ Had my lessons become monotonous to the point of incessant repetition, the kind that required no future planning because the same lesson was being taught on a weekly basis?
- ♦ Had I failed to prioritize, causing time to be spent on less important matters?

♦ Were the futures of my students as important as whatever it was I would have preferred to be doing instead of planning?

Was spending time planning part of the original bargain you thought you had made when you signed on the dotted line? Was it the price you were willing to pay? Had you bargained for something this time-consuming and tiring? If your answers are "no," do you realize that you are in the wrong profession? Are you willing to change your priorities in order to remain a part of the profession? If so, read on.

Avoiding the Mistake

An effective lesson always begins with the end in mind. What are my goals? What are my objectives? (What will my students know and be able to do by the end of the lesson?) A well-planned lesson consists of several basic parts:

1. **Focus:** What will I do to "hook the fishes" so that I can begin reeling them in? How will I motivate and inspire interests in them? Will I tell a story? Will I relate the topic to their lives in some way? Will I allow them to share their own stories? Will we role play? Will I include an element of surprise, or will this day begin like all of the others?

2. **Modeling:** How will I teach the new concept? Will I show, tell, and model? Will I model again? And again? And again? Will I question the students while modeling the skill? Will I invite input and critiquing? Will we compare the skill to one already taught? Will we build on that previously taught skill? How?

3. **Guided Practice:** Will I allow the students to try it? Will I guide and assist them through this process? How will I do that? How will I know when they are ready for the next step? Can I assume that they will all be ready at the same time? What will I plan for those who need extra help and time? How will I determine which ones need extra help and attention? (Will I be assessing throughout this process?)

4. **Independent Practice:** What activities will I plan for independent practice time? Will they be assessed? How? Will all students be assessed in the same manner? How will I know which need more help than others? How will I know if the independent practice was effective? Were all students engaged and on-task? Were they inquisitive? Were the activities creative enough to sustain interest and attention?

5. **Closing/Review/Summation:** How will the lesson culminate? Review and reinforcement? Assignment? Questioning? Discussion? Preview of what is to come next? Will there be a finished product to evaluate?

Bottom Line

Failure to plan is a plan for failure, and none of us would deliberately plan for failure. Planning is arguably the most difficult part of teaching, because it is so multifaceted.

- ◆ It requires time, patience, diligence, and determination.
- ◆ It requires impeccable prioritization and organizational skills.
- ◆ It requires an understanding of what true, effective teaching really is and how it is executed.
- ◆ It requires an understanding of each year's students and the realization that no two groups are alike.
- ◆ It requires an understanding of individual needs and how to address them.

Effective teachers will tell you that their hardest work is done during the planning phase. They will also tell you that effective planning is the only way to ensure a great time teaching! Teaching is extremely fulfilling, but not if you're dealing with the repercussions of poor planning: disorganization and chaos.

First, set aside and plan time for planning. Then, plan for effective teaching. Everything else will fall into place. Have you planned tomorrow's lesson yet?

I had a plan to make a plan
My New Year's Resolution
But since I failed to plan the plan
This still was no solution.

The plan did not materialize
I did not follow through
First you have to plan the plan
Then do what you plan to do!

—Elizabeth Breaux
(From *Real Teachers, Real Challenges, Real Solutions,* 2004)

I Am the Teacher

I am the teacher, the trusted adult
Have faith in my skills and I'll show you results
I'm driven, determined, I'll go to all lengths
To champion my fervor, exhibit my strengths

There aren't many puzzles that I cannot solve
When faith and tenacity fuels my resolve
No hurdles I've met could suppress my convictions
The most they've accomplished were minor restrictions

I know where I exit and where you come in
The end of my rope is where your rope begins
I'll complete every task and fulfill obligations
Before seeking you for my final salvation.

—Elizabeth Breaux

Mistake 15: Misusing the Administration

Defining the Mistake

The most successful and productive schools are those where all faculty and staff work as one entity. From principal to teacher to clerk and from custodian to cook to bus driver, the dividing lines are seamless. All are comfortable in their roles and self-assured in their own worth and place. They are confident in their value as an intricate part of the bigger picture.

These are the schools where the slogan "Children First" is personified. The fundamental belief is in the power and the obligation to mold the child. Decisions are made for the good of all but with the focus on the children. Selfishness and pettiness are thwarted and replaced by altruism.

And then … everyone awakens from the dream!

Can you imagine the school where everyone actually does work in unison? Where no one is used and no power is abused? Where all actually do the job for which they were hired and remove themselves from matters which are none of their concerns? It seems shameful that this is only a pipe dream. It should be a reality were it not for those who will not allow it to be. Do you know any of them? Are you one of them? Do you really want to be?

I am not, have never been, and have no intention of ever becoming an administrator. I spent many years teaching and then several years as a curriculum coordinator in a middle school. It wasn't until I became a curriculum coordinator that I learned the true role of the administrator, even though I had assumed that I understood it all along. It was then that I learned about the plethora of responsibilities, the incessant demands, and the awesome responsibility for accountability. It was not until that time that I realized just how badly their positions are abused by those who don't understand their own roles.

- ◆ I've seen bus drivers expect the school-based administrator to police their buses.

- ◆ I've seen cafeteria workers, office personnel, custodians, and teachers (all adults) bring personal differences with peers to the administrator to resolve.

- ◆ I've witnessed, daily, the same teachers summoning the administrator to their rooms to handle "emergency" situations. I observed that most were NOT emergencies.

- ◆ I've eyed the enormous stack of discipline referrals as it grew from day to day and watched administrators shuffle through them using valuable time that could have been better spent. I knew that on many of the referrals, teachers had elicited the help of administrators for such things as getting students to stop talking, do their homework, bring their materials, stay in their desks, and so on. Those are jobs that I had always assumed, as the teacher, were my own responsibilities! Wasn't I the one hired to be the teacher? Wasn't I the adult in the classroom? Weren't they my students, under my care? If the administrator had been responsible for all of these other undertakings, why had I been assigned there? Was I even needed?

The principal is the school-based leader and is ultimately responsible for all that occurs. He/she is the one upon whom we rely when we have exhausted all efforts. The principal is the last resort when all else fails.

I am the adult in my classroom; therefore, I am capable of making the adult-like decisions necessary to keep my environment well-managed and trouble free. If/when at any time I have depleted my "arsenal," then and only then will I turn to other resources. Until then, *I am able and qualified to handle typical situations such as*

♦   talking;

♦   failure to complete homework assignments;

♦   off-task behaviors;

♦   gum-chewing; and

♦   minor dress code violations.

I am not and should not be required to handle flagrant situations which require outside assistance, such as

♦   physical fighting;

♦   possession of a weapon;

♦   use of threats; and

♦   flagrant disrespect.

These are instances where removal from campus through suspension and/or expulsion is usually merited. I, the teacher, must hand that over to the administration for that determination to be made and for the necessary steps to be taken.

Example of the Mistake

Mrs. Houston was very well-known on campus. She was the teacher whose classes could be heard coming from far and away. She was the teacher whose students disturbed all classes within the immediate vicinity. She was the teacher who seemed incapable of managing children. The children literally ran the classroom.

Mrs. Houston's management plan consisted of issuing idle threats and punish work, screaming, using sarcasm, and issuing office referrals, office referrals, and more office referrals. Mrs. Houston often complained that the administration did nothing to discipline the children. The administration often complained that Mrs. Houston did nothing to manage her classroom. Because of failed management on her part, little teaching and learning were accomplished in Mrs. Houston's classroom.

On a typical day, Mrs. Houston summoned an administrator to her room several times. On a typical day, several children were referred to the office by Mrs. Houston for disciplinary action. They were referred for reasons such as

♦ excessive talking;

♦ failure to "do their work"; and

♦ disrespect. (An observer would have noted that the majority of disrespectful remarks made by the students were in direct response to Mrs. Houston's disrespectful words and gestures.)

In spite of the disciplinary action taken by the administration, nothing will change until Mrs. Houston makes some changes. Changes in herself!

Correcting the Mistake

If you remember from chapter 2, "Attempting to Control," Mrs. Houston would first need to gain control of Mrs. Houston before a controlled environment could emerge within her room. Her practice of relying on the administration to control the environment in her classroom was doomed to failure. The only one in control of that was Mrs. Houston. As long as she continued to relinquish her power to the administration, her weaknesses would continue to be exploited by the students.

To gain control of her class, Mrs. Houston must gain control of herself. Her past tactics have obviously not worked. Committing to changes in her own behaviors is within her control. These are the ones she must seize. They are the only ones she controls.

There's an old saying, *"If you do what you've always done you'll get what you've always gotten."* If what you've been doing is not producing the desired results, change is critical!

Avoiding the Mistake

Relying on the administration to manage the day-to-day operation of individual classrooms is unrealistic and abusive to the position. Just as an administrator's responsibility is to manage the overall operations of the school, it is the teacher's responsibility to manage the overall operations of the classroom. Only in extreme cases, as listed in the Defining the Mistake section, should the teacher relinquish power to the administration.

Teachers are the managers of their own domains. Teachers must preserve their own authority by controlling their own actions and reactions to situations. This is the only way to avoid the mistake!

Bottom Line

Teachers must squelch the urge to solicit the help of an administrator in matters that are and should be under the realm of the teacher's responsibilities. Habitually sending students to the office is a sure way for teachers to inevitably surrender their own power. It sends the message to the students that the teacher has lost control. That will be the ultimate demise of the classroom. Effective teaching and learning will no longer be feasible.

When I walk into a classroom and observe a teacher handing back stacks and stacks of graded papers, I have to wonder whether or not the students even remember taking those tests and quizzes. What I do know for certain is this: They won't be learning from the mistakes they've made if they can't remember making them!

—Linda Nance
Middle School Principal

Mistake 16:
Delaying Feedback

Defining the Mistake

By definition, the term "feedback" refers to a return to information in order to correct or to evaluate it. In the classroom, we take that definition to new heights. The act of giving feedback is performed as another method of teaching. Feedback time is of greatest value when mistakes are rectified, understood, and remembered. Why do we want to make certain that students remember the mistakes? So that they don't make them again! In other words, in order to rectify a mistake, I must first make one. In order to learn from my mistakes, I must be given the opportunity to review, correct, and evaluate them. Only then can true learning, retention, occur.

When mistakes are utilized and viewed as an opportunity for teaching, they are not made in vain. Instead of discouraging the mistakes, teachers should view them as opportune teaching moments. The window of opportunity for learning from mistakes is short-lived. The student must remember the mistake and how and why it was made in order to evaluate it and make necessary changes.

The best teachers are also in tune with the human need for feedback. Regardless of age, we all want to have our jobs, roles, and so forth, evaluated for efficiency and effectiveness. Without it, we become complacent and stagnant. Don't we teachers all want and expect immediate feedback after being formally observed by an administrator? I know I did.

Students want feedback immediately after a graded assignment (test, quiz, etc.) has been completed. They will often ask teachers for an approximate time frame between completion and return. The best teachers will do whatever it takes to get those back today, if possible. If not, no later than 1 day later and NEVER more than 2 days afterward. Delaying feedback will only lessen the chance for the learning opportunity to be effective.

Recently, I was conducting a 3-day training for a large group of teachers and administrators in Louisiana. These adults were taking the course in order to become certified assessors in the Louisiana Teacher Assistance and Assessment Program (LaTAAP), which is a certification process that all new teachers in the state must complete before becoming state certified. During that 3-day training, prospective assessors are given three different tests, all of which must be passed before the participant can obtain certification. As their trainer/instructor (and former classroom teacher), I know that immediate feedback is imperative if mistakes are to develop into knowledge. I also know that these adults want to know their scores! They want to know their scores for the same reasons that students want to know theirs. Invariably, when beginning one of the three tests, the participants will ask two questions:

1. How many can we miss and still pass?
2. When will we know our scores?

Sounds familiar? Are these the same two questions asked by our students in our own classrooms? Are we adults any different when it comes to wanting feedback immediately?

I always score the tests during the lunch period so that I can return them before the end of the day. The group members appreciate that. So do our students.

If providing timely feedback on a given test is not viewed as being important and/or useful, then this question should be asked: "Was the test necessary?" In other words, how will the information gained from the test results be used? If several students fail the test, are the results used to guide future lessons (reteaching, etc.), or are they simply used for evaluation purposes? The best teachers know that they are used for both!

Feedback is most effective when given immediately. Only then can the outcomes be optimized and the distinct purposes accomplished:

1. Reinforcement of what has already been learned.
2. Rectification of mistakes made so that learning can occur.
3. Plans for reteaching, if necessary, can commence.

Examples of the Mistake

Mrs. Copier's students are never short on grades, but are usually lacking in knowledge. They are always quite busy but rarely effectively learning. Mrs. Copier spends a lot of time planning lessons and grading papers, but little time actually teaching. A typical week in Mrs. Copier's class looks something like this:

Monday:
♦ Introduce new concept.
♦ Hand out the week's packet of worksheets for students to begin working.

Tuesday:
♦ Students continue work on this week's packet of worksheets.
♦ Mrs. Copier scores/grades last week's packet of worksheets.

Wednesday
♦ Same as Tuesday.

Thursday

♦ Complete all worksheets and hand in.

Friday

♦ Test on material "learned" that week.

♦ Return and go over last week's test and packet of worksheets.

By the time the test and graded worksheets are returned from the previous week, another packet has been completed. Students barely remember the content. Interest is nil other than in the actual score, since this determines and affects their averages. Mrs. Copier does take time to examine and correct errors on the returned work, but the window of time where opportunity for reteaching can be effective has expired.

This example is a bit extreme but not uncommon. Let's take a look at one that, regrettably, is more ordinary.

Mr. Procrastinate has a motto: "Never do today what can be put off until tomorrow." He has learned that some things can even be postponed indefinitely. "If you put it off for long enough, people sometimes forget."

Because Mr. Procrastinate neglects to plan effective lessons, he must resort to filling the class time with busy work. He has learned that most students will complete the assignment if they know that it will be graded. Since Mr. Procrastinate realizes that many of the assignments are of little relevance, scoring and returning them to the students is often delayed and sometimes postponed indefinitely. Once too much time has elapsed before he returns the assignments, the students have forgotten the material. Mr. Procrastinate's trash can is filled with these forgotten assignments.

So let's think about this. Mr. Procrastinate neglected to teach, students were left to their own devices when completing the assignments, and feedback on the assignments was rarely given and never in a timely fashion. Did learning occur? Is Mr. Procrastinate really a teacher?

Correcting the Mistake

Following are a few tips that can be used to identify and rectify the problem. When giving a graded assignment, test, and so on, consider the following questions before proceeding:

1. What is the importance and value of it, and what purpose will it serve?

2. Will feedback be given in a timely manner, while the information and interest in the information is still fresh in the students' minds?

3. How will the feedback be delivered in order to utilize it as a teaching tool?

4. How will the results guide future instruction?

Definitive answers should be given to all of these, or the assessment may not be a valid one.

Avoiding the Mistake

I utilized what I called my "One Day Rule." I would never allow myself more than 24 hours before providing feedback to students. In order to adhere to my own rule, I shared it with my students at the beginning of each year. If you want to be kept accountable, count on your students to do it!

Extended projects or other lengthy, graded assignments were always broken into smaller parts which would eventually culminate in the whole. I had learned that when students are given lengthy assignments in small increments, the assignment/project seems much more doable to them. Feedback on individual portions must be provided in a timely manner. When grades on individual portions are later combined for an overall score, students get a clearer picture of the relationship between the parts of the assignment. Also, when a teacher uses feedback time to evaluate the caliber of the work, the overall result is one of higher quality. Grades are better. Learning has been achieved. What else is there?

Through the years, I learned that any assessment that cannot be used as a teaching tool and as one that will guide further instruction is basically useless. If, as with Mr. Procrastinate, throwing it away and forgetting about it is an option, it must have been meaningless in the first place. Graded assignments should never be used as time-fillers, lest we squander and lose valuable teaching time. It can never be recaptured.

When testing is viewed as a teaching tool as well as an evaluation tool, mistakes are more readily avoidable. As a teaching tool, the results are an essential component of the ongoing teaching and learning process, so postponing feedback is counterproductive and thereby avoided at all cost.

Bottom Line

When we forget the importance of feedback, the feedback becomes unimportant. Delayed feedback loses its effectiveness and usefulness. Golden teaching opportunities are missed when feedback is suspended. We all want feedback, and we want it NOW! "Now" is the time when it is most relevant and most practical. Don't procrastinate. The students are waiting!

> *I didn't know the answer, so I didn't raise my hand*
> *But the kid across the room who could answer on demand*
> *Had both hands in the air so high that I really couldn't see*
> *Why the teacher didn't call on him, but set her eyes on me.*
> *"Oh please," I begged in silent prayer, "don't let her call my name—*
> *For I am not as smart as he, and I will be ashamed."*
> *The teacher, much to my surprise, changed the question in midflight*
> *To one that she was certain I could surely answer right!*
> *So with enthusiasm I answered really loudly*
> *And nowadays, I must admit, I'm feeling rather "proudly"!*

> —Elizabeth Breaux
> (From *Real Teachers, Real Challenges, Real Solutions*, 2005)

Mistake 17: Discouraging Participation

Defining the Mistake

To impede participation in any way is the last thing we would ever intentionally do in our classrooms. In fact, lack of participation in some classrooms, and with certain students in particular, is a chronic complaint among teachers. Ironically, many of us actually discourage and prevent the very participation which we are struggling to acquire without ever realizing what we are doing.

I learned the hard way, at the expense of my students, that my reaction to incorrect responses was the key to the future participation of those students. My reply to an incorrect student response could either encourage or prevent future participation. My words are that powerful.

In the previous chapter on the necessity of timely feedback, we discussed the fact that mistakes are an important part of the learning process. They are inevitable and highly useful. We use them to build upon. In order to foster growth through them, we need for students to know that it is okay to make them! If we discourage the mistakes by making students uncomfortable, we inevitably discourage participation, the very thing that we are trying to encourage! (Are you totally confused and discouraged now?)

My sister, Annette, a former elementary teacher, created a mantra that she taught to her students every year at the beginning of school.

Mistakes Are Great!

Mistakes are great—we just can't wait
Till someone makes another
Each time they do, they help us to
Learn more and discover
So let us take this mistake
And learn a lesson from it
For when we do, we're able to
Get up each time we plummet!

The message is a simple one: we learn from mistakes, so there is absolutely no shame in making them. The shame, sorry to say, often comes from the teacher.

Example of the Mistake

The words of a teacher are powerful and can have lasting effects. Following is a list of powerful, yet harmful, replies made by teachers to incorrect student responses:

- "If you had been paying attention you would have known the answer to that!"

- "We've been talking about this for weeks. Where have you been?"

- "You don't know? What do you mean 'you don't know?' "

- "Every third grader should know that. Do you need to go back to second grade?"

- "That was an easy question. What are you going to do with the hard ones?"

- "You obviously didn't do your homework."

Had I been one of the recipients of those teacher responses, I would have NEVER participated again. In fact, I would have been so busy mulling over the teacher's words that my mind would have been incapable of absorbing anything else.

There are teachers who will actually call on students who they know are not paying attention just to embarrass them. If you've ever had that done to you, you know the feeling. Teachers do it with the intention of "teaching them a lesson." Unfortunately, this "lesson" is not one that will encourage future participation. It may be the best way to discourage it indefinitely. The classroom needs to be a safe place. It must assume an environment where students are safe from bodily and emotional harm. We teachers are the protectors and insurers of that safety. Let us never be the ones to infringe on it.

Correcting the Mistake

A teacher's response to an incorrect answer from a student should be calculated. It should be one that makes the incorrect response okay to make, leads the student to the correct response, and encourages future participation. Let's look at some teacher responses to incorrect student answers that would promote further participation.

- "That not quite it, but I think I know what you are thinking. In fact, I had never thought of it that way."

- "That's an interesting answer. It's not the one I was looking for. Let's look at the question again, and I'll explain it a little more clearly."

- "Close, but not quite there yet. Keep thinking, you're on the right track."

- "Let me give you a few more minutes to think about it; that was a difficult one."

In regard to embarrassing a student with the intent of encouraging future participation—forget it! That one never works. For the teacher who feels the need to "win" at the cost of the student, the endeavor will always result in a questionable victory for the teacher. What about the student?

If a student is obviously not paying attention, it is the job of the teacher to help him/her return to task without resorting to embarrassment or sarcasm. Sometimes, proximity can be the key. Moving in the direction of the student may possibly be all that is needed. Other instances may require that the teacher "hang out" near the student for a while. (This will make most students uncomfortable enough to get them back on task ... quickly!)

Sometimes, words of encouragement are necessary:

- "That's a great idea for a topic sentence! Please let me know when you have finished the paragraph. I can't wait to read it!"
- "I see you are struggling a bit with this one. What can I do to help you?"
- "Take your time. I will be in here at recess today, and we can work on it then if you need more time." (That one always gets them back on task!)

Encouraging words will encourage participation. Discouraging words will not. Which ones will you use?

Avoiding the Mistake

Getting students to participate is a process. It should begin on the first day of school, when you are developing a good rapport with your students. It is always a good idea to spend some time discussing the topic of participation with your students. Put them at ease by letting them know that "Mistakes Are Great!" Without them, learning would not occur.

I used to take the opportunity to give them some really silly examples that helped to make the point. I'd ask those questions such as "What happened the first time you tried to dress yourself, to ride a bike without training wheels, or to color a picture?" I'd then ask how many of them today were able to dress themselves without help, to ride a bike without training wheels, and to color within the lines. This always led to some interesting discussions. It also made this point: *Without mistakes, learning would not be possible.*

A tactic that I used frequently when returning a graded assignment worked like a charm. While scoring the students' papers, I kept my roll book open to their names. After scoring each individual paper, I'd write at least two of the numbered items that students had answered correctly next to their name. In that way, when going over it in class the next day, I could make certain that individual students were called on to give answers only to items that they had answered correctly on the graded assignment instead of ones they had missed. The more that I did that, the more voluntary participation I began to receive.

Bottom Line

If you want your class to be one where students are on-task and participation runs rampant, do the following:

♦ Make certain that your lessons are hands-on, where students are actively involved in the learning process.

♦ Put your students at ease from day one by letting them know that mistakes are necessary and welcome.

♦ Let them know that everyone makes mistakes. It's the way we learn. It's natural and normal and nothing to be ashamed of doing.

We must help our students to lose their fear of being wrong and must NEVER be the ones who cause them to be fearful of being wrong. We must instill in them, through our responses to them, that nothing was ever learned without making mistakes. Make no mistake about it, "Mistakes Are Great," as long as we correct them and learn from them.

A Teacher's Oath

I, the teacher, promise to take your child and hold him securely under my wing. I will love, nurture, care for, protect, and teach him to the best of my ability. I will share his sorrows and pains, his joys and his successes. I will be proud of him and of the job that I will do to assist him on his journey. I will choose to like him even when he is difficult. I will choose to differentiate between "bad actions" and "bad people." I will never become a victim of him, nor will I ever allow him to be victimized by me. I will be firm, kind, fair, and consistent. I will treat him as my own, giving him no less than the best that I have to give. I will become allies with those who love him the most, his parents, and bond with them in their endeavor to mold him into all that he is capable of becoming. At the end of the year, I will send him on his way without regret, for I will know that I have done my small part in giving him the tools that he needs to become a productive, contributing member of society. I will cry as he leaves me, both tears of sadness (for I will know that my job has been completed) and tears of joy (for I will know that I completed it well).

—Elizabeth Breaux
(From *How to Reach and Teach ALL Students—Simplified*, 2007)

Mistake 18:
Sacrificing the
Parent-Teacher Alliance

Defining the Mistake

Show me a parent who does not care about the well-being of their child and I'll show you a monster. If what many teachers say is true, that "parents just don't care about their children anymore," then there must be a lot of "monsters" running around out there. The reality is that an overwhelming majority of parents really do care about their children; we teachers merely disagree with the way that some of them demonstrate it.

Assuming that the issue is simply one of semantics, we must agree that parents do care. They do love their children and want only the best for them, even if they don't always behave as though they do.

Parents can be a teacher's greatest ally. When parents are on our side, great feats can be accomplished. When parents and teachers become allies in the molding of the child, accomplishments can be achieved that might not have been made single-handedly.

On the other hand, parents can become a teacher's most dreaded foe. When we perceive them as adversaries, we feel limited in our ability to help students perform at their potential. I have often heard teachers, myself included, complain about a lack of parental involvement. I've heard them say things like:

- ◆ "The parents don't care anymore. It's not like it was when we were young."
- ◆ "I can't even contact anyone. The numbers we get are either bogus or have been disconnected."
- ◆ "Education is just not at the top of their lists."
- ◆ "Have you ever met his mother? How can you expect any more of him?"
- ◆ "Open House was a joke. The parents who needed to come didn't show up."

The fact is that in many cases, if teachers want parents to become involved, teachers need to take the first steps. Stop waiting for the parents to come to you. Many will not. Many are actually afraid of becoming involved or don't really know how to become involved. Many parents will tell you that they only hear from the school when there is a problem. If we teachers wait to call home only when the call is in reference to a negative behavior, then we are setting ourselves up for failure to establish a cooperative alliance with parents. Furthermore, we are often afraid to make that call. It's not comfortable or easy, and we are often happy when no one answers!

We do have the power to change this. We can initiate the contact any time—the sooner the better—and in reference to positive behavior. If we do that, we are ensuring two things:

1. It will be a positive, pleasant call, and the parents will feel that they know us and that we are on their side.
2. If we ever need to call in reference to a negative behavior, they will answer the phone and be willing and happy to help.

The old saying, *"You never get a second chance to make a first impression,"* so suitably applies to the parent-teacher alliance. The only way to make certain that a first "chance" meeting is a positive one is to arrange it. Set it up. Plan it meticulously. Control the circumstances. Call/e-mail parents and/or orchestrate meetings before negative situations arise. This is the only way to ensure that the first impressions are positive ones. When doors are open, relationships can be built. Do it quickly, before the doors slam in your face!

Example of the Mistake

Mr. Browbeat doesn't need help from parents. He assumes apathy in them and therefore exerts no effort in trying to form alliances with them. His communications with parents have all been of a negative nature. Since he contacts parents only when negative situations become acute, the ensuing meetings are usually more destructive than helpful. This, of course, affirms his belief that *"Parents don't care."*

Jeremy is Mr. Browbeat's most incorrigible student. Jeremy is often late for class, he seldom does his homework, and he is frequently off-task. Mr. Browbeat has tried sarcasm and cynicism on Jeremy to no avail. He has belittled and demeaned Jeremy in front of his peers. Again, no success. He has referred Jeremy to the office administration where Jeremy has been assigned to lunch detention and Saturday school. Nothing works. When asked by the administration whether or not he has consulted with Jeremy's parents, Mr. Browbeat gives his generic response: *"They are of no help because they obviously don't care."* (In other words, "no," he has not contacted the parents.)

The principal arranges a meeting between Mr. Browbeat and Jeremy's parents. The meeting commences with both parties already taking a defensive approach. Mr. Browbeat reads his list of Jeremy's faults to the parents. Jeremy's parents counter with excuses. Mr. Browbeat displays his displeasure. Jeremy's parents become more defensive. Mr. Browbeat retaliates. Jeremy's parents storm out in anger. Mr. Browbeat claims victory; his "point" has been proven.

Correcting the Mistake

Because parents' perceptions of their children's teachers are initially and largely based on the child's perception of the teacher, Jeremy's parents already viewed Mr. Browbeat with disapproval. Mr. Browbeat's reputation preceded him, and his ensuing behaviors were always in accordance with parental expectations. The only person capable of mending those viewpoints was Mr. Browbeat, yet he continued to behave in a manner in line with his reputation.

If Mr. Browbeat were ever to turn over a new leaf, he will need to commit to doing the following:

- Adjust his attitude toward his students and their parents;
- Take an inventory of his methods and determine which were providing the desired results;
- Begin making positive parent contacts early in the school year; and
- Maintain ongoing communication with parents.

During the following summer the principal arranged for him to attend inservice training on establishing positive relationships with parents. He began by creating a positive contact log and committing to using it. He gathered "tips for getting parents involved" (see the next section, Avoiding the Mistake) from colleagues and actually implemented the procedures.

Avoiding the Mistake

This section comes from my book, *How to Reach and Teach ALL Students—Simplified* (2007, pp. 45-47).

Tips for Getting Parents Involved

- Commit to making a positive parent contact for every student you teach, during the first few weeks of the new school year.
- Divide the number of students you teach by the number of days that you would like to commit to making calls home. For example, if you teach 50 students, give yourself about 2 weeks (10 school days). You would have to call five parents per day in order to finish within the 2-week time frame. If you teach a total of 25 students (as you might if

you are a self-contained elementary teacher), you may want to contact five parents a day and finish in one work week.

- On the first day of school, verify the students' contact information that has already been computer generated. Sometimes the phone numbers, e-mail addresses, and physical addresses have changed. Students are very willing to give you the correct information during those first days.

- Commit to using part of your before-school time, your planning time, your lunch time, your after-school time, and so forth, during the days that you will be calling home. However, evenings should be open for calling only those whom you were unable to contact during the school day.

- Make a list of positive commendations that could be used for any student. Before making the call, you can pick one or two (or more) that apply to the given student. Your list might look something like this:

  - Your child is very polite.
  - Your child is very cooperative.
  - Your child obeys school rules.
  - Your child follows procedures willingly.
  - Your child is very helpful to me and to other students.
  - Your child is usually on task.
  - Your child is a hard worker.
  - Your child has a lot of potential.
  - Your child is attentive.
  - Your child does his homework.
  - Your child is organized.
  - Your child is creative.
  - Your child enjoys reading.
  - Your child apologizes when he/she makes a mistake.
  - Your child is a good leader.
  - Your child works well in groups.
  - Your child makes friends easily.
  - Your child respects authority.

- Plan your dialogue. One thing you don't need is to be on the phone for 30 minutes with each parent. I have found that beginning the conversation with something like this works beautifully:

"Good morning Mrs. Johnson, this is Ms. Breaux, Jason's history teacher. I apologize if I am disturbing you. I know that you must be quite busy, so I won't keep you long."

By telling the parent that you won't keep them long because you know they are busy, you are indicating immediately that this will be a quick, unobtrusive call. You can then proceed to complete the conversation by saying something like this:

"I just wanted you to know that I am so happy to have Jason in my class this year. What a hard worker he is! He has done everything I've asked of him so far. He is really attentive too, and always on task. I'm just calling to let you know that you are more than welcome to call me at any time and/or to come in for a conference. My planning period is from 9:30-10:30, and I'm also available before or after school any day. We're planning a field trip at the end of the month and could use some help. If Jason's organizational skills are any indication of yours, we could definitely use your help!"

- Once all initial calls are made, plan for subsequent positive calls. You could commit to calling one parent per day with "good news" for the remainder of the year. Even if you teach a large number of students, that could still mean that each parent will get more positive calls than they've received cumulatively throughout the duration of their child's years in school.

- E-mails can be equally effective. Just make certain that each is personalized and not of a generic nature which makes it highly impersonal.

- Create a list of ways that you could elicit their help and use this on your subsequent contacts. Once they get to know you, they are much more likely to volunteer to help out. If you give them the impression that you welcome and need their help, they will feel needed and more likely to offer their services.

Bottom Line

When parents are on our side, great feats can be accomplished. When we perceive them as adversaries, we limit our ability to help students perform at their potential. If we truly want to stimulate parental involvement in our schools and in our classrooms, we must make these commitments:

- We must choose to believe that all parents truly care about their child's education, regardless of whether or not we feel that their actions portray this.
- We must choose to believe that we have the power to combine forces with even the most reluctant parents.
- We must realize that many parents' experiences with the school have been only negative and that this is what they expect.
- We must commit to being the one who initiates the positive interaction and know that it is not likely to occur otherwise.

By choosing to be relentless in our endeavor to involve parents, we teachers are guaranteeing that we as well as the parents and the students will reap the benefits. We cannot force parents to become more involved in the education of their children, but we can open the welcome door and invite them in. We must believe that we have the power to increase parental involvement and make it a positive experience. We must not allow ourselves to become negative, incredulous cynics, for if we do, we all lose. Just ask Mr. Browbeat!

When life threw me a hardball
And daddy moved away
I tucked it deep inside my soul
Since words I couldn't say
But seething deep within my core
And dying to emerge
This little girl becoming me
Just looming on the verge
Of reason fading in the far
Illogic in the near
Becoming one my parents
And my friends began to fear.

My teacher didn't notice
She didn't seem to care
She wouldn't heed my warnings
She didn't even dare
When I said that I wouldn't
She showed me that I could
When I displayed indifference
She must have understood
When I became uncaring
Lethargic, in despair
When all my words and actions
Should have proved I didn't care
She didn't let me off the hook
But held me close at bay
She saw behind the mask, I'm sure
And soon peeled it away.

—Elizabeth Breaux

Mistake 19:
Believing the Façade

Defining the Mistake

How often have you heard comments like the following (or similar to them) made by fellow teachers?

- ◆ "The students these days don't care about anything or anyone but themselves."
- ◆ "Education is not important anymore."
- ◆ "They don't want to be here, so how can we teach them?"
- ◆ "They don't appreciate anything."
- ◆ "We give them too much these days, and they just expect more"

That last one is particularly disturbing to me. I believe that when we refer to the students as being *"given too much,"* we are more or less referring to material things. The real problem is that many don't get nearly enough of the necessities in life that are in no way material: the intangibles that mold us into who we are and what we become. Is it true that many of them *"expect too much?"* Probably. But it depends on your definition of "too much." Do they expect more material things than we did when we were their ages? Of course! There are far more material things out there that didn't exist when we were younger!

Is it fair to say that an *"education is not important to them"* and that they *"don't want to be here?"* I'd say that's a relatively fair statement. It's of no more importance to them today than it was to most of us when we were their ages. I don't know about you, but I was the average "good" student. Had you asked me on any given day whether I'd prefer to go to school or to stay home, I would have picked the latter. Was that because education was not important to me? No. It just wasn't all that important on that particular day! I couldn't see the big picture. My biggest "picture" spanned about 5 days: yesterday through the following weekend. Anything beyond that was of little concern or value to me. It's supposed to be that way. I was a kid! Just out of curiosity and to prove the point, pole your faculty and ask how many would like to have this Friday off. How many do you think would forego that luxury? Is it because they don't value education for the children? I doubt it.

Is it fair to say that *"they don't care about anything or anyone but themselves?"* The message that they send is precisely that. Adolescent years, especially, are the "me" years. The mask they wear is clearly intended to portray the "it's all about me" persona. Deeply seated within them (for those who are willing to take a closer look) are the same cares and concerns that we all harbor. The similarities between the adult and the child are simply distorted by the façade.

We are the adults. We should know the difference between "what is" and "what is exposed." We should not be fooled by the façade. If we take away the masks we'll notice that all children are basically the same, with the same wants, needs, and desires as everyone else. If we believe the façade, everyone loses.

Example of the Mistake

Brandy was the class outcast. She was clearly overaged and overgrown for a seventh grader. She didn't have many close friends, a fate she had obviously chosen. Her character was clearly known and understood by all. It said:

- ♦ "Stay away from me!"
- ♦ "I don't need anyone!"
- ♦ "I don't care about anyone!"
- ♦ "You can't hurt me!"
- ♦ "I will hurt you if you mess with me!"
- ♦ "I don't care about school, and I don't want to be here!"

Brandy's reputation preceded her every year. Teachers were on guard. If Brandy was in your class, it was not going to be a good year.

Brandy spent most of her school days sleeping. When Brandy wasn't sleeping she was either just waking up or getting ready to nap. She always looked exhausted. She was allowed to sleep as much as she wanted. Teachers had learned that it was much easier "not to mess with her." When Brandy slept, they could teach. So the cycle had continued:

- ♦ Brandy slept.
- ♦ Brandy got punished. She spent much of time in lunch detention, but that never seemed to bother her. She preferred that to mixing with others at recess. The intended punishment was actually a reward. Teachers, however, just kept punishing her.
- ♦ Brandy failed.

Brandy was 3 years behind in grade level. There was no hope for her. Teachers just bided their time with her and then sent her to the next teacher.

Correcting the Mistake

It was the first day of school when Brandy first entered my classroom. I had seen my roster of students and knew that she would be in my class. She would definitely be a challenge, but I was ready. Let the "contest" begin!

Brandy's reputation had been quite accurate. She sat as far to the back of the room as she could. She spoke very little, if at all, to anyone. She would have remained off task the entire year had I not found ways to keep her involved.

I knew that treating Brandy differently from everyone else was what she was used to and what she expected, so I made certain not to do that. I made a contrived effort to find the positives in her on those first few days of school, and there really were some.

1. I asked if she would mind being my "second pair of hands and eyes" since she was in the back of the room near my supplies area. I kept her during recess one day, knowing that she would not object, and told her that I needed some help. The fact that she was older and "more mature" than most of the others made her my first choice. I showed her where everything "lived" in my room and made her responsible for disseminating and collecting supplies, in addition to several other everyday jobs.

2. I had noticed that when I was able to keep her on task with her class work, she was quite smart. She picked up on concepts very quickly. I complimented her and called her mother immediately. I told her mother that this year would be a turning point for Brandy. That was a promise I was determined to keep.

3. I had noticed that Brandy really did have trouble staying awake. I would watch her trying to pay attention, her head bobbing from side to side as she would try to keep from dozing. I talked to her and told her that I was extremely impressed with her brilliant mind. I told her that I noticed how quickly she absorbed new material. I told her that I was aware of her struggle to remain alert during class and offered a solution. I had cleared an area in the back of the room near my counter. I told her that if she ever felt herself nodding off, she could move to that area with her materials, and that she could stand in the back to continue her work. I told her I thought this would help her to stay awake and she agreed. Notice that I didn't insist on this, but presented it to her as an option after telling her what a terrific job I thought she had been doing.

Brandy began making use of the option to stand. No one seemed to notice or mind. The fact is that no one else would have dared make a comment about anything that Brandy did for fear of bodily harm.

As Brandy and I developed a rapport, we spoke one day about her sleeping problem. She revealed to me that she NEVER slept at night. She said she couldn't. Her two brothers were in and out all night. One of them played a musical instrument and played it at all hours of the morning. Her mother was in an abusive relationship with an alcoholic who wreaked havoc on the household. She didn't have a bedroom but slept on a sofa that opened into a bed in the middle of the ongoing chaos. She said she had learned that there were always going to be teachers who would allow her to sleep, so she had taken advantage of that. She also said that she could nap on most afternoons, since she was often home alone at that time. I told her that she was welcome to come to my room at recess every day in order to rest, if she needed to.

To make a long story short (and it is a very long story), Brandy did not fail that year. In fact, she did so well on the state exam that she was able to skip the eighth grade and move on to the high school, where she was among others who were of the same age.

I think of her often and wonder what ever happened to her. I hope that her high school teachers refused to believe Brandy's façade and, instead, looked more deeply into what was a beautiful young human being, with dreams and aspirations, trying to overcome many obstacles that few of us can comprehend.

Avoiding the Mistake

Brandy helped me to become a far better teacher than I had ever been. She opened my eyes and revealed to me that no one is ever exactly what he or she appears to be. I tell the new teachers with whom I work today the story of Brandy. I tell them to look beneath the mask, but that first they must believe that masks exist. The child who professes lack of concern is the one who feels it the most.

Bottom Line

We must never be fooled into believing what appears to be. We can never allow ourselves to be deceived by what appears to be a pretty package. Sometimes, the very worst scenarios and conditions come wrapped in ribbons and bows. We need to seek the truth, have compassion, keep expectations high, and we will reach and teach the child.

> *Mistakes I've made, both grave and small*
> *(In that I'm not alone)*
> *But the ones that harmed me most of all*
> *Were the ones I failed to own.*
>
> —Elizabeth Breaux

Mistake 20: Refusing to Acknowledge Mistakes

Defining the Mistake

If you do not make mistakes, you are not human. If you do not acknowledge your mistakes, you cannot learn from them. If you cannot learn from your mistakes, you cannot grow. Mistakes are natural and integral to life. They help us grow and excel. They keep us from stagnating

Complaining, blaming, and excuse-making, as discussed in chapter 9, are common methods of shifting responsibility for mistakes toward someone else. When I fail to recognize my own faults, I concede my power to fix them.

There are those who have made the same mistakes, year after year, decade after decade. We all know them. They are firm believers that the methods they use are valid, but that the responses they are receiving are faulty. They blame the response on the responder, who in the case of the classroom teacher, can be anyone from students, to administrators, to parents, to fellow teachers. As long as there is a refusal to acknowledge mistakes, the vicious circle will continue.

Students (children) are notorious for blaming others, a common trait among students that teachers loathe. We expect and demand that our students take responsibility for their own actions and mistakes. We should do no less ourselves. When we model the skill of acknowledging mistakes, we teach and confirm that mistakes should not be viewed as obstacles, but as common, necessary, stepping stones toward learning. When we make it okay for us, the adults, to make mistakes, it becomes more acceptable for the students.

Example of the Mistake

A young teacher came to me, crying and threatening to quit her job. She just couldn't take it anymore. The students had no respect and, due to their poor behavior, could not be taught. Class work was rarely completed, homework was seldom done, and papers were never returned. After trying everything in her power, she was met with worsening behavior from her students. There was nothing more she could do. She had conceded defeat.

I was able to convince her that she was not powerless, that she had not come close to exhausting all of her options. She asked if I would spend a day with her, observing her classes, and, of course, I agreed. Without going into great detail, here are a few of the "teacher's mistakes" I observed:

- The teacher seemed obviously frustrated and aggravated as she stood in her doorway greeting her students. Her greetings sounded something like this: "Hurry up!" "Where have you been?" "Don't come in here talking today!" "I am not in the mood for that today!" "I am not tolerating it today." "There is an office referral on my desk waiting for you. Don't make me use it!"

◆ Several students arrived late. The teacher asked them where they had been. The students gave beautifully contrived stories. The teacher told them to be seated. There was no obvious penalty for being tardy.

◆ Several students did not have class materials. Again, she asked the "why" questions; and the students, as they will always do, gave the typical, untrue excuses. The teacher continued to "teach."

◆ After approximately 15 minutes of unsolicited and unwarranted movement of students around the room, she demanded that they stay in their seats. For the previous 15 minutes the movement had not been acknowledged by the teacher.

◆ There were several instances where the teacher admonished a student for poor behavior; the student retaliated, and the teacher engaged.

This list goes on and on.

The next day, she and I met and discussed every detail of the observation. I assured her that every one was fixable, if she would agree to acknowledge that her behaviors alone were the ones that should be targeted for renovation. She did agree, although reluctantly at first.

Correcting the Mistake

The first thing I suggested was that she film herself. I shared with her that it had been the best thing that I had ever done to better myself as a teacher. It had revealed things that I was not even aware that I was doing. She did, and she and I watched the tape together. She said that it felt as though she was watching someone else. She was immediately able to recognize flaws that she did not know existed. This was the beginning of awareness and acknowledgment for her, and the repairing phase was poised to begin.

My next suggestion was that she should observe other teachers. I recommended that she observe her own students in other classes. Often when observing unfamiliar students in a classroom where the teacher is an accomplished classroom manager, the observer is quick to attribute the good behavior to the teacher's good fortune of having a class of "good" students. The observer is thus compelled to think that this would never work with her/

his students. I accompanied the teacher on her first two observations so that we could compare our opinions of what had transpired and why.

Finally, I suggested that she ask to be observed by several others on campus, administrators and fellow teachers, and be willing to listen to their observations and incorporate their ideas.

Avoiding the Mistake

At first the young teacher in the previous example was unwilling to acknowledge the mistakes as her own. She had been blaming the students (and everyone else) for the mistakes and then wondering why the mistakes continued, over and over, the same way, every single day! Her willingness to be more open-minded helped her discover that SHE had been making the same mistakes, over and over, the same way, every single day! By acknowledging her own mistakes, she was able to fix them. By becoming more willing to fix her own mistakes, she began acquiring more appropriate and gratifying responses from her students.

Her experience is the epitome of what can happen when mistakes are acknowledged, addressed, and used as learning tools. Once this is accomplished, the same mistakes are unlikely to recur, and new ones can be addressed! And there are always new ones to be addressed, but that's how we grow—by learning from our mistakes!

By remembering previous mistakes and taking the necessary steps toward amending them, we can avoid making the same ones over and over again. Oh, and don't keep reinventing the wheel! Use your peers, especially those of us who have been around for a long time. Let us share with you the most commonly made mistakes so that you can avoid them!

Bottom Line

There is no proven way to avoid making mistakes, but why would we want to even if there was? What we want to avoid is the mistake of failing to acknowledge mistakes. Without acknowledgement, mistakes cannot be corrected. Without being corrected, mistakes lose their power to teach powerful lessons.

If you do not make mistakes, you are not human. If you do not acknowledge your mistakes, you cannot learn from them. If you cannot learn from your mistakes, you cannot grow.

A Teacher Cared For Me

When I was hurt and crying
From having fallen down
A teacher came and took my hand
And helped me off the ground
She dried my tears and tied my shoe
She brushed away the sand
She said that I could walk with her
Then gently took my hand.
When I had been offended
By the kids who'd done me wrong
A teacher said she'd been there
It wouldn't last for long
She said that I should stand my ground
Endure what was to come
That I would be the stronger for it
In the longer run.
When my first love no longer felt
What was inside my heart
And spoke to me those dreaded words
That one says when they part
My teacher didn't say a word
She simply closed her eyes
And said that she could feel my pain
But soon it would subside
She said that pain is cut in two
When shared with someone else
One day a friend would call on me
And I should share myself
I think about those teachers
And the one I've grown to be
I know it was, in part because
A teacher cared for me.

—Elizabeth Breaux

Conclusion

Teachers—

You pave the road that carries your students to their futures. Lay it carefully, but not flawlessly. Provide assistance, but include obstacles and hurdles along the way. For each hindrance, afford reason, purpose, and example. Teach them that the road of life is fraught with error, but for each blunder there is a greater purpose, a purpose that, without acknowledgement of error, reveals no gain. Teach them that, and you have taught them the greatest lesson of all.

My wish for you is that you and your students make LOTS OF MISTAKES, but that you accept and learn from each, so that you become stronger and wiser with each passing year.

Best regards,
Liz